The Ankh symbolises the unity of Osiris and Isis. Osiris was murdered and rose to heaven. As a god in heaven, Osiris miraculously impregnated his wife, Isis, who gave birth to Horus. The manner of Isis conception led to her being described as a perpetual virgin, the Isis Mery. Ancient Egyptians believed that when Osiris returned to rule the Earth, he would resurrect the bodies of the dead and they would be reunited with their souls. Elements of these, already ancient, beliefs may have influenced gospel writers in the 1st Century AD.

....

This book is dedicated to the millions of individual people that, over the centuries, have been tortured and murdered simply because their beliefs differed from those wielding power at the time.

The Truth Will Set You Free

THIRD EDITION

Part one

God, Enki, Ra/Marduk & Yahweh

Proof of a divine Creator and clues to the real identity of Yahweh

GLYN THOMAS

Quintology Publishing
www.truthpublications.co.uk

Copyright © 2023 by Glyn Thomas & Gregory Thomas

All rights reserved, including the right to reproduce this work in any form whatsoever, without permission in writing from the publisher except for brief passages in reviews or in citations and references.

Printed by Ingram Spark and affiliates – Lightning Source UK Ltd, Milton Keynes, United Kingdom (see inside back for this copy). Third Edition, published September 2023.

Paperback ISBN: 978-1-7384439-2-5
Ebook ISBN: 978-1-7384439-3-2

Typeset, layout and cover design by Gregory Thomas
www.gregthomas.design

Contents

1. Challenging aspects of conventional Christianity
2. The Universe – spontaneous or a deliberate creation
3. Life – what did God create?
4. The contrasting characters of Yahweh and Jesus
5. The history of history
6. Evolution is the primary tool of God
7. The creation of the Torah
8. What is the Genesis story of creation?
9. Who was Abraham?
10. Israelites in bondage, or, enslaving the Egyptians?
11. Who was Moses?
12. Who is God in the Torah?
13. Modern maps show Sinai in the wrong place
14. Amen – origin and meaning
15. Did Jesus believe the Old Testament?
16. The Nature of Jesus – God, or man or both?
17. Where did the idea of a Triune God come from?
18. Original conclusions
19. Conclusions – God as a singularity

Appendix: Key family members of the ancient 'gods'
Index
Biblical references
Bibliography
Books in this series
Symbols used on covers in this series

1

Challenging aspects of conventional Christianity

1.1 Christian theology seems long overdue a major upgrade – to remedy erroneous ideas adopted in the early centuries of the church but more importantly to recognise specific fundamental information about our universe and ourselves that has been revealed to us in the past few decades.

1.2 This third edition of what is my original book in this series reflects new discoveries in the topics explored and the evolution of my thinking on what exactly God might be. To enable readers of this series to follow the impact of my research, debates and personal thoughts, I have added a new concluding Chapter 19 speculating about the origin, form, characteristics and objectives of God. To enable comparison with the first phase of my journey from 2013 to 2016, I have retained the original conclusions, as Chapter 18. What is interesting is how little of the original content I now see as invalid – the change has come from a wider perspective and from embracing far broader possibilities. You, the reader, will be judge of whether I have made progress!

1.3 Another significant addition is in Chapter 3, where new text explores the progress made through the development of Covid vaccines. For the first time, new vaccines exploited our knowledge of how our DNA operating system works. The breakthrough results from being able to replace the relatively haphazard and unpredictable editing using CRISPA-Cas9 to the pinpoint precision provided by Prime Editing – a technique first reported in October 2019, just before Covid 19 was first detected. Prime Editing enables new genetic material to be stitched into a specific location in our DNA – Covid 19 vaccine packages comprised recognition code to identify Covid cells and new weapons to kill off such intruders. Whilst not widely publicised, these mRNA vaccines both updated our core DNA, which genetically we now will pass on to our descendants whilst also providing us with a medication devoid of side effects. This new technique will soon transform our approach to treating illness – more in Chapter 3. Another important threshold we stand at is the discovery of key components of RNA in samples recovered from asteroids – pointing to the possibility that life is a natural development across the cosmos, again more details in Chapter 3.

1.4 When you look around and think about how the world was created and how life emerged – most people would agree there are only two possibilities – either the whole of existence is a freak accident or a supreme intelligence acted to create our universe. The idea that we and our universe could be the result of some freak natural event quickly falls apart when one delves into atomic physics. The early chapters of this booklet are my attempt to explain in laymen's terms the evidence of intelligent design (revealing the 'hand of God') – NOT in the design of humans or other species as promoted by Fundamentalists but much more fundamentally in the very formulae that rule the atoms across our cosmos. My studies suggest to me that our Creator appears to be somewhat of a mathematician. Most of the signs the Creator reveals to us are mathematical – from the mathematical constants in the incredible equations that control cosmology to beauty in all its manifestations. Many of the mathematical formulae that govern key physical relationships in the cosmos have utterly exquisite values seeming set to exceedingly precise numbers by a polymath genius. Whether considering physical beauty, art or music – all are resolvable into numbers. Many studies have found what humans recognise as beauty can be mathematically expressed as symmetry. If a 1000 people are asked to rank a file of faces in terms of beauty – the ranking invariably corresponds to the level of symmetry revealed in each face. I think this a logical conclusion because mathematics is a truly universal language – unlike any other with the exception of love – is this a mere coincidence ?

1.5 A supreme intelligence, acting as Creator, is usually referred to as God. Mankind has long struggled to identify and define God, to discern God's plans and character, and not least the purpose and role of humanity. Our Creator appears to have deliberated, carefully and thoughtfully, to develop the genetic code which endows us with intellect: optimising our intellect is probably pleasing to God (after all, that must be the intention of the design); alternatively, wasting our intellect or leaving it idle, is unlikely to be pleasing to God. Therefore, we should apply our intellect to live well, generate resources and use our resources to love others.

1.6 Early man's knowledge of the cosmos and of biology was basically limited to what he could see – without specialist equipment or the knowledge that would be gleaned from the use of such equipment. The earliest known ancient civilisations, the Sumerians and the Egyptians, seem to have progressed a bit further – gaining a good understanding of our solar system and could very accurately predict future eclipses. Records of their calculations of eclipses and planetary dawns, dating back between 4000BC and 2000BC, demonstrate their knowledge of heliocentricity – i.e. they knew that the planets orbit our star. In the Prequel to this series, we found evidence of a far earlier civilisation, dating back before the large meteor impact around 10765BC which led to global memories of "the Flood". Remnants of this earlier civilisation managed to bestow some of this knowledge on post Flood cultures in Sumeria and Egypt. In relatively recent times, from 334BC, those invading the Fertile Crescent lacked this knowledge – under the Greeks and the Romans, cosmology relapsed to a much cruder belief in a flat earth with a covering dome upon which the Sun, Moon and other celestial bodies moved on almost fixed tracks. The Apostle John, writing in Revelations, obviously believed this – as he seemed to view the stars as being like lightbulbs which an angry God might cast down to smash upon a sinful world.

1.7 Over the past millennia, well intentioned theologians have constructed complex rules and interpretations of belief – leading to religious dogma becoming a prime generator of bigotry. Initially, those raising doctrinal arguments were declared heretical and any deviant believers were usually hounded to death. Later, doctrinal differences led to schisms, followed by intra-faith warfare just as bitter as between different faiths. Fragmentation, particularly of Christian beliefs, has led to myriad denominations – and the resulting cacophony of dissenting views has contributed to the growth of disbelief and atheism. All three Abrahamic faiths (tracing origins from Abraham's descendants) have been affected to a greater or lesser extent by fragmentation. It is assumed that these monotheistic faiths have long fixated about there being one God – the definition of monotheism. But how true is this?

PART ONE: GOD, ENKI, RA/MARDUK & YAHWEH

1.8   Certainly for Islam this holds true – Islam stresses that God is unique, tawhid, and describes God as unknowable and unimaginable, therefore God cannot be either material or spirit – because we can rationalise spirits whilst God is beyond our understanding. In Islam, 'spirit' is used as a term to classify non-material beings such as angels and their lesser brethren, jinn. Indeed, Jesus explanation of God being 'spirit' maybe understood better as 'a pervasive power' rather than a non-material entity.

1.9   Mainstream Christianity believes in a Trinity, a complex confection which actually dates back only to Emperor Constantine's Council of Nicaea in AD325. As this series explores in detail, all quotations of Jesus statements describe a deferential relationship with God, whom he referred to as a father whom he obeyed, worked for and who had granted him extensive authority. The early Roman church conflated 'Khristos' (Greek for 'messiah') with 'Son of God' and accordingly concluded that Jesus was literally God's son. But this ignores Jewish scripture, which records hundreds of officially recognised messiah's – none of whom were ever remotely considered divine. As researched for this series, the biblical evidence does not support Jesus ever being anointed a messiah in compliance with the Old Testament definition, although it seems he may have been eligible. Jesus own followers in the original Nazarene Church did not believe Jesus was God but that he had been granted divine authority.

1.10 John 1:1, traditionally understood in English to read "in the beginning was the Word, and the Word was with God and the Word was God" is, in the Greek original, stating that Jesus is divine but not that Jesus is God. John reflects contemporary Greek belief that when God created humanity, he also created an intermediary, the Logos, who would communicate through speech to convey God's messages to humanity. John's contemporaries would read John 1:1 as stating "in the beginning when God created humanity (i.e. not when God created our universe 13.82 billion years ago, but very recently when modern homo sapiens emerged – indeed, female mitochondria indicates this was just c172,000 years ago), God also created a Communicator, 'the Logos', the Logos was close to God and was his representative, and the Logos was divine". In Greek, John 1:1 states "and the Logos was a god". Official Catholic publications record that belief in Jesus divinity was something that grew in the second half of the first century – i.e. it was not a belief held by the church founded by Jesus contemporary followers – the Nazarene church, led by Jesus brother, James, for 29 years after the resurrection.

CHALLENGING ASPECTS OF CONVENTIONAL CHRISTIANITY

1.11 So, to summarise the above, it would seem that Jesus and his Apostles, certainly according to John, believed Jesus was divinely empowered and authorised by God but not that Jesus was God. 'Son of God' is, at least in part, a misunderstanding by the Roman Church of what the Greek 'Khristos' (i.e. messiah) meant – this is clear from many Christians referring to Jesus as 'The' Messiah rather than as "a" messiah. Indeed, very few Christians are aware that: firstly, 'messiah' is an office that one requires hereditary descent to be eligible for; secondly, that there were always two messiahs (a king messiah and a priest messiah); and, thirdly, that anyone eligible to become a messiah only became a messiah under Mosaic Law if anointed with a special mix of oils and herbs (sort of ancient salad dressing) by the High Priest – and, another of the 613 mitzvah which comprise the Mosaic Law, sets out grave punishment for anyone falsely claiming to be a messiah. The idea that Jesus was anointed messiah by a High Priest prior to or during his ministry sounds pretty unlikely.

1.12 In conclusion, whilst it does NOT affect my view that Jesus has divine authority over mankind, nor my acceptance of his teaching, there is evidence that the message of salvation has been deliberately twisted. Further, claims that Jesus is God, is the Son of God, and even the "Only" Son of God – are not only contradictory but when considered carefully lack credibility even in the context of the bible. All our records of Jesus teaching show clear, direct and powerful messages designed for easy understanding by his contemporaries. The Gospels make no reference to Jesus claiming to be the Creator, or part of a Trinity, everything points to Him being instructed by, and obedient to, the commands of his 'Father' – a term I suggest is linked to Jesus central message of love and a focus on supportive relationships. Indeed, in Greek and Roman culture it was common for bright young adults to be legally adopted, or to seek the patronage of, wealthy individuals whom they then acknowledged as 'father' and whose family name they then adopted.

1.13 The biblical record of Jesus sayings (the red letters), texts generally regarded as highly authentic, quote Jesus clearly stating on a number of occasions that "God is spirit" – which makes the Trinity a bit weird – The God Spirit, the Holy Spirit and Jesus? Jesus description implies God is a force rather than an entity. A force can more easily be omnipresent, existing to some extent everywhere – including within humans. Paul, whose writings comprise about 50% of the texts admitted into the New

Testament, makes deferential reference to a text ruthlessly destroyed by the Catholic Church in which Jesus in quoted as stating: "your Spirit belongs to God but your Soul belongs to me". This statement has enormous implications and is explored in Part 4 of this series.

1.14 If we look more closely at Judaism, it is clear that Yahweh was the god of the Israelites only, other peoples worshipped their own gods and no effort was ever made to convert them. Reading the Old Testament one may conclude that the gods were each allocated their own territories – Jacob's seed (descendants) was Yahweh's inheritance, for whom the land of Canaan had been 'promised'. Again, when David is chased out of Israel by Saul's forces, David complains to Saul that by chasing him out of Yahweh's territory, David will be forced to worship the god of the foreign land into which he has fled (1 Samuel 26:19). Yahweh was believed by the Israelites to be more powerful than other gods (hardly surprising) and very jealous of his people, often referring to them as his 'inheritance' (based on Deuteronomy 32:7-9) but definitely Yahweh was one of many gods.

1.15 Looked at objectively, Jewish beliefs seem to be wishful thinking – far from ruling forever, David's line lost, and never regained, 10 of the 12 tribes at only the second succession. Ten tribes were deported to Nineveh after only 300 years and Judah lasted only another century before deportation to Babylon. The great return to Jerusalem after Cyrus defeat of the Babylonians attracted only 4% of the Jews then living in Babylon. Thereafter, during the following 2,500 years the Jews have enjoyed being an independent self-ruling country for less than 200 years. Firstly, from 165BC until 64BC the Hasmonean Kingdom between Greek rule and Roman rule. Later, Roman rule switched from Rome to Constantinople, then Israel became part of the Muslim caliphate, then it was taken over by the Crusaders (who also massacred the Jews in territory they conquered), before reverting to Moslem rule and finally, under the British Mandate until 1948 from when a second period of self-rule has been established. So much for Yahweh residing in Jerusalem forever – it seems like the other ancient gods, Yahweh simply passed away or maybe was killed in a battle with the Chaldeans (Babylonians) shortly after 600BC.

1.16 This series will review a great deal of evidence supporting the interpretation of Yahweh being one of the family of ancient Middle Eastern gods, identifying who these gods may have been and confirming that Yahweh

CHALLENGING ASPECTS OF CONVENTIONAL CHRISTIANITY

was one of their number. One might conclude Judaism is not monotheistic, only that it unsurprisingly claims that its god is best. Most theologians would admit that only post Babylon (c530BC) would most Jews begin to restrict their worship to Yahweh. Old Testament texts, written by Yahweh's prophets and priests, naturally promote Yahweh but at the same time make many references to other people's gods. The evidence indicates the Israelites were far from monotheistic, they worshipped a number of gods – many idols have been recovered from Israelite graves and ruins; the books of Judges and Kings tell of frequent and widespread worship of Astoreth and Baal; Solomon built niches for many 'foreign' gods in the Temple; Ezekiel complains of the women wailing for Tammuz in the Temple and indeed a shrine to Tammuz has been excavated in Bethlehem that is contemporaneous with Jesus time.

1.17 When I was around 10 years old, I speculated that God might be a force similar to electricity. Today, I think God might be what is termed 'Dark Energy', which accounts for over 2/3rds of the mass energy of our universe. The anthropomorphic viewpoint of conventional Christianity implies the Godhead is a person and thus incredibly microscopic in relation to his creation. In speculating that Dark Energy could be God's Spirit we can more easily consider our universe as God's plaything. Whilst Dark Energy comprises 68.3% of the mass energy in our universe, matter (all the stars and planets that we can detect) makes up only 4.9% – that God might be Dark Energy is a rather more humbling thought than traditional images of a Father Christmas!

How was conventional Christianity established and Jesus original message partially lost and distorted

1.18 In order to gain some perspective, it is worth considering the broad history of Christianity. Within two centuries of Jesus time on Earth, Christianity had spread right across the Roman Empire and far beyond – to Ireland and across India. Many view the conversion of Emperor Constantine to Christianity as the big break which elevated Christianity to the state religion of the Roman Empire. However, in AD325 at the Council of Nicaea, Constantine managed to force the early Church leaders to agree a new dogma merging Pauline Christianity (itself significantly differing from the beliefs of Jesus' own Nazarene Church) with the cult of Sol Invictus. Ironically, the Roman 'Sol Invictus' was derived from the ancient god Shamash – which even Biblical evidence suggests was the very same entity as Yahweh. Some key tenets of Christianity stem not from Jesus but from the decisions of the Council of Nicaea and later Church Councils. These aspects are explored in detail in Parts Three and Four.

1.19   The Council of Nicaea enabled the church in Rome to establish a unified religious structure which devoted a significant proportion of its energies and resources to rooting out all and any deviations from the new dogma that the Council had codified. All deviations from the new dogma were deemed heretical. Actions taken to root out heresies were often very brutal, involving probably millions being mercilessly killed because they were found with a copy of a banned text or had spoken of beliefs no longer tolerated by the Church. For example, Catholic armies tasked with eliminating French Cathar heresies in the 13th and 14th centuries, took to herding villagers into their parish church, barricading the doors and then burning entire communities alive – using the justification that God would know his own and save the souls of those who were innocent.

1.20   Most Christians are aware that the early church battled with what is described as "deviant" dogma, or heresies. We know huge numbers were killed for their heretical beliefs and we generally acknowledge that the Catholic authorities went too far in persecutions such as that conducted by the Inquisition. But what is less widely known is that the numbers of martyrs created by killings carried out by the Catholic Church are many times the number killed under the edicts of Roman Emperors prior to Constantine. Typically, under Papal edicts, entire families were killed because one person was found in possession of a banned text. There is widespread acceptance that these persecutions constitute a bad stain on the Church but almost no knowledge of what these heretical beliefs were and why were they so ruthlessly rooted out. Increasingly, academic research indicates that views labelled heretical by the Roman church were generally the majority viewpoint prior to being suppressed – and that such repression was mainly to protect and promote the political power of the Roman Church.

1.21   The destruction of early Christian texts represents the most successful censorship campaign in the history of the world. So much so that when caches of early texts were unearthed in the Twentieth Century, only a minority of the texts bore titles that we had any record of. What these texts reveal is the original message of Jesus and by comparison we can

CHALLENGING ASPECTS OF CONVENTIONAL CHRISTIANITY

see just how far his message and teaching has been twisted to create dogma which endows religious authorities with political power over its adherents. Part Four of the series sets out to reveal the authentic Truth as taught by Jesus and recorded in texts that were later regarded as heretical and methodically destroyed.

What existential threat does conventional Christianity face today?

1.22 The infamous Donation of Constantine (Emperor AD306 to AD337) purported the transfer of all authority over the lands of the Roman Empire and the Sees of Antioch, Jerusalem, Alexandria and Constantinople to the Pope as a gift in recognition of God healing Constantine's leprosy. First used in negotiations by Pope Hadrian I in 778, the Donation came to be wielded by successive Pope's as their authority to approve the coronation of any earthly ruler within the realms of the former Roman Empire. The 'Donation' gave the Pope enormous political authority:- magnifying claims to be vested with the authority of God in relation to earthly matters courtesy of a lineage of office traced from Saint Peter, the Donation was used as authority to choose who was crowned king. By extension, it became a Papal matter whether one king could attack another; a kingdom which allowed heretical views to prosper was at risk of invasion at the command of the Pope.

1.23 Monarchs quite liked the approval of God's representative on Earth, giving rise to the concept of the Divine Right of Kings – a king could do no wrong if appointed by God and, if he did do wrong, then he was only accountable to God. The story of David's aversion to killing the wicked Saul, despite being presented with many opportunities, because Saul had been appointed by God, was seen as the guiding example. Accordingly, regicide was believed to be the most heinous crime – England was deeply shocked when Charles I was beheaded at the order of the English Parliament in 1649. At the same time, this event stiffened the backbones of Catholic monarchs to support requests from the Vatican.

1.24 In 1440, an Italian priest, Lorenzo Valla, proved conclusively that the Donation of Constantine was a forgery (as it used terms dating only from the 8th century) but remarkably the Vatican managed to suppress the evidence until 1517. Naturally, this news was then seized upon by Protestants as further cause for their schism from Rome.

1.25 This centralised authority and unified dogma enabled Christianity to survive through the Dark Ages after the fall of the Roman Empire. The Renaissance occurred when the Christian faith was firmly established as the European cultural norm. The introduction of the printing press by Gutenberg in 1522 meant that the global spread of European culture, building colonial empires, came complete with unlimited copies of the Bible to establish Christianity. However strong or weak the faith of any individual, almost everyone attended church each week, across the entirety of Europe up to the religious border with Islam.

1.26   It is worth considering two factors which, whilst largely absent today, exerted a controlling influence on people's view of life until quite recently. One was destroyed by electricity, the other by social developments. Until the spread of electricity, everyone was profoundly affected by the nightly presentation of the glory of the galaxies – a staggering sight reminding them of biblical references they heard every Sunday concerning the majesty of God. Instead of seeing the Milky Way every night, most people now have their eyes glued to a screen. The other factor is respect for authority, which has also now largely evaporated over the past hundred years. Under Roman jurisdiction, only Roman citizens enjoyed any sort of legal rights, other people whether free or slave were subject to arbitrary whims of the local Roman authorities bent on the twin aims of eradicating dissent and extracting taxes. In the subsequent Christian domains across Europe, people's lives were subject to the commands of those appointed by God – the priest appointed by the Church headed by God's appointed representative on Earth and the officials appointed by the King, who also ruled by divine right. So, to complain or to dissent was to challenge those granted authority by God.

1.27   The exposure of the Donation as a fraud, and the spread of Protestantism (which severed entire countries from the control of the Vatican) led to the demise of the divine right of kings and the eventual replacement of ruling monarchies by democratic politicians. I know that is a very broad, sweeping statement, but it neatly paraphrases half a millennium of European history! Certainly, removing God from the equation led to citizens taking a more critical view of those wielding authority. A world in which you and everyone else was at church every Sunday and the local lord of the manor had a title bestowed by the divinely appointed king, was progressively replaced by a king and a pastor who had both rejected the authority of the Pope and a society where everyone had some civil rights under which they could challenge those in authority. Political control passed from the king to elected representatives of the people. Opinion research repeatedly shows the collapse in the level of trust people have in all representatives linked to authority – from church leaders (child molestation); politicians (greed and personal ambition); lawyers; bankers; even doctors (bribed to oversubscribe by pharmaceutical businesses) – all have seen the level of trust, and hence respect, totally collapse over recent decades.

1.28 The Catholic Church, an immensely wealthy and powerful organisation, reacted strenuously to counteract any developments which challenged the orthodox beliefs which it had established. In countries where Protestant views were resisted by the monarchy, the Vatican managed to exercise a large measure of political control until quite recently – e.g. over divorce and abortion in Ireland. When the Vatican heard about Copernicus heliocentric model of our solar system in 1533, it was identified as a major threat to the conventional earth centric model of creation that derived from Genesis and the Church acted accordingly. Scientific discoveries over the past 400 years have increasingly challenged the articles of dogmatic faith. Our knowledge of the cosmos, molecular chemistry, biology and history has grown exponentially. Sadly, the tendency of organised religion has been to treat each discovery as an affront and try to reject anything that contradicts dogma. This has resulted in the schism between secular life and the sacred. It has led to the 'head in the sand' arguments put forward by the 'Inerrants' – those firmly believing that the Bible is the very Word of God and therefore must be inerrant (devoid of any error) in its entirety.

1.29 The force of the traditional argument, that a learned priest appointed under the delegated authority of God has told you things that you should just accept and believe, in faith – is no longer effective. Respect for all elites has plummeted, civil rights and print media have exposed widespread scandals involving appalling behaviour, compounded by leadership which acted only to cover up such sins.

1.30 The problem for established religion is that trust in church authority has been eroded whilst general levels of education and knowledge have been rising – leading more people to question biblical inconsistencies and dubious dogma. Specifically, even a relatively rudimentary understanding of four key disciplines (cosmology, molecular chemistry, biology and history) seriously undermines traditional dogma and inevitably leads to the rejection of purported Biblical truths and, by extension, Christianity, by growing numbers of people.

1.31   As I have found, it does not take much academic training to get to grips with the basics of these disciplines and discover the truth. The most exciting element of truth is that humanity now has clear evidence proving our universe was created by a supreme intelligence. What has also been revealed is the method of creation – God writes rules, amazingly complex precise mathematical laws embedded in chemical equations. Earlier generations assumed the process of creation was effected by God as if by magic, by miracles God spoke things into existence. Now we know better, we can understand the rules controlling atomic physics, set down by an intelligence beyond our understanding, which led to the evolution of our universe over billions of years to the point at which we now exist. It was very refreshing to hear Pope Francis state in October 2014 that "God does not do magic".

1.32   The next two chapters contain some quite technical detail – but please persevere as the rewards are truly great. Chapter 2 addresses cosmology, expanding on the section in the first edition, and after writing this second edition, I was delighted to find one of my key sources, Martin Rees, Britain's Astronomer Royal, had been awarded the Templeton Prize. This prize is awarded to those helping to bridge the gap between science and religion. Chapter 3 is material new to this edition and explores our growing knowledge of DNA. Imagine my surprise when I read that Dr Francis Collins, director of the US National Institutes of Health, who had led the team who first mapped the entire human genome – has also been awarded the Templeton Prize.

1.33   A skin deep understanding of any one of the four disciplines referred to above gives sufficient insight to appreciate the awesome majesty of the Creator – and at the same time raise serious doubts about the entity referred to as Yahweh in Jewish scripture and assumed to be God in the Christian Old Testament. Therefore, whilst there are strong grounds to believe in a Creator and massive evidence to support that argument; a similar weight of evidence undermines theological support for the Israelite god of the Old Testament, Yahweh, as being that Creator. Like the followers of any 'pagan' deity, the Israelites developed rituals, songs and poetry to praise their concept of god. But a careful analysis of biblical evidence of the character, statements and actions of Yahweh (and according to Genesis, his progenitor, El Elyon) show such an entity cannot have created the Earth, let alone the immensity of our universe. Moreover, love is hardly Yahweh's strongest character trait. Jesus stated clearly a number of times: "God is Spirit", by comparison Yahweh was dependent upon the daily provision of roast meats (with pleasing aromas and after careful butchering and removal of excess fat which was to be disposed of far away, outside the Israelites camp); shewbread (which Yahweh always insists should be devoid of yeast, no doubt because he had an allergic reaction to yeast) and also – surprising quantities of wine.

1.34   Additionally, whilst evidence from the Bible itself shows Yahweh cannot be the Creator God and definitely not the Father that Jesus prayed to and obeyed, the Bible is also full of clues as to exactly who Yahweh was. The evidence indicates that Yahweh was initially a son of the Lord Most High, El Elyon, who was named Nannar by the Sumerians and Sin by the Akkadians. Sin was the city god of both Ur (where Abraham's family originally lived) and Harran (now in southern Turkey, where Abraham's family moved). Sin was linked to the moon and known as the young bull – hence significance of the crescent moon and the golden calf. Exodus records the auspicious day that the Israelites stopped and camped for Moses to ascend the mountain – "it was the very day of the new Moon" – hence the Jewish Mosaic festival to worship the new moon. The same ancient god, Sin, also got into the Koran and is immortalised on the dome of every mosque and on the flags and currencies of most Moslem states. As we explored in the Series Prequel, ancient Middle Eastern civilisations did not believe gods were immortal, just that they enjoyed long lives but could be killed in battle or an accident. So, a millennium after Abraham, by the time of the Davidic monarchy, Yahweh (previously associated by the Israelites with Nannar) had evolved to being associated with Nannar's son, Shamash – in Hebrew, Psalm 84 baldly states: "Yahweh is Shamash, Shamash is Yahweh" – English translations manage this embarrassing statement by describing God as being our sun and providing warmth and light.

1.35   Hence my personal conclusion that the Old Testament is nothing to do with the Creator God and nothing to do with Jesus. In Part Three of this series, I describe in detail the biblical records of Jesus rejecting every tenet of Judaism (except love). Moreover, when examined, there is ample evidence that the so called 'prophesies' pointing to Jesus that are claimed to be in the Old Testament are almost all quickly revealed to be fake (mistranslations, changed wording), non-existent (as with the prophesy that the Messiah would come from Nazareth) or very weak. Therefore, my conclusion is that Christianity needs to junk the Old Testament, re-examine the evidence which points to Jesus original teaching and recognise God's prolific revelation concerning his Creation that, with recent immense leaps in our knowledge, we can now begin to understand.

Aspects of Christian theology that need updating

1.36   We need to objectively study our constantly expanding knowledge of how our universe has evolved and the rules governing physical matter, dark matter and dark energy to discern as clearly as we can the work of the supreme intelligence that designed those rules. We need to apply the same dedication to determine the rules to create life and the origin of DNA. These studies will inform our view and belief in the Creator who deserves the title of God.

1.37   Jesus in his human form seems to be unique. Exhaustive textual analysis of his teaching as recorded in the four Gospels suggests the 'red letters' sections are largely authentic and transmitted to us in something close to their actual form. However, from examination of the "heretical" texts, it appears that key elements of Jesus teaching were excised by the Catholic Church in the 4th and 5th centuries – whilst spurious wrappers were also added, including the nativity stories. Jesus teaching is at once quite simple and also very profound – opening a window whereby we can begin to understand God.

1.38   Of fundamental importance is that we re-evaluate the orthodox linkage of Jesus and his teaching to the Jewish scriptures and Yahweh. As addressed in this series, there is plenty of evidence in the statements by Jesus that he rejected every single tenet of Judaism – one can hardly claim that the command to love God means loving the god of the Israelites – obviously every religion thinks it a good idea to love God!! Jesus message was that we should show we love God by loving everyone else, at first sight seems extraordinary – and certainly not the core feature of Judaism.

1.39   The early church seems to have assumed that because Jesus appeared as a Jew, Judaism was his heritage. Certainly Jesus used the Jerusalem Temple to teach – but we forget that this was also 'city hall' as Judea was a theocracy – as were all the early civilisations in the Middle East. Jesus divinity, effected I believe by a hefty dose of Spirit, enabled him to read people's minds and somehow instruct human DNA to effect emergency repairs – viewed at the time as Jesus performing miracles. Jesus appeared to know the Jewish scripture by heart, again presumably courtesy of the Spirit. Careful analysis of the Gospels shows that Jesus teaching contradicted every key aspect of Judaism and also that he pointed out errors in the Pentateuch. If this sounds radical, a fuller explanation is given in Part Three.

1.40 It is instructive to learn that the very first Christian Bible contained only Luke and the Pauline letters bound into a single book. The editor, Marcion (AD85 to AD160), first produced the book around AD144. Marcion, having access to all the texts subsequently destroyed by the Catholic Church, specifically excluded what we term the Old Testament entirely, saying it was nothing to do with Jesus teaching. Indeed, the creation of the first Bible incorporating both New testament texts as well as what was termed the Old testament came only as a reaction against Marcion – 175 years later. This was prepared when the Roman Church was battling to determine its dogma, and is known as the Codex Sinaiticus, dated to cAD320.

1.41 It is clear that various edits and embellishments were made to the original texts of some New Testament books – these are explored in detail in Parts Three and Four. Removal of such extraneous material, no doubt originally intended to boost the credibility of the gospel message, would be a sound move as it now has the opposite effect. To informed minds, the embellishments lack credibility and raise doubts about the authenticity of Jesus and his message. Therefore, I also propose a re-evaluation of the books of the New Testament to show more clearly what is generally judged to be original from what we have evidence has been edited, added or, admittedly more difficult to identify, what may have been deleted. We should also look at incorporating texts wilfully destroyed by the Roman church – if Paul quoted the Gospel of Thomas in the same manner as he quoted parts of the Torah – by prefacing quotations by "as it is written", then surely it should be reappraised and included? Similarly, both Jesus and his brothers, James and Jude, all quote from the first book of Enoch – which the church excluded.

1.42 When taking time for a much closer study of the Bible the biggest issues for me were the deep character differences between the 'God' of the Old Testament and Jesus – despite the official church concept of a triune God forcing us to consider them being of one homoousios, being of the same essence. For some time, the most worrying concern for me remained the dilemma between on the one hand what I found revealed about God in the Old Testament and on the other hand its numerous prophesies supposedly foretelling events concerning a future Messiah – which seem to be fulfilled during Jesus life on earth. But again, I found that all is not quite what it seems at first reading.

1.43   This series also includes the results of studying many articles supporting the position that the Bible constitutes the Word of God and therefore must be inerrant (without error). The arguments supporting this position are uniformly self-serving and invariably use circular logic within the Bible to justify itself. Indeed, I was very relieved to find the arguments for inerrancy to be so weak as to greatly strengthen my belief that I am on the right track!

1.44   Anyone, like this author, who has identified scientific evidence of a divine creator and gained an understanding of the original teaching of Jesus finds it difficult to understand the role of Yahweh from the Old Testament. Most committed Christians seem to rely heavily on the Bible being the Word of God and most simply ignore anything that would seem to contradict the foundation of their belief. This probably reflects an understandable concern that admitting any single statement is wrong would open the floodgates to further questions. Sadly though, it would seem that the Bible has for many become a crutch to support their belief in God rather than supporting evidence of why they believe in God. It is also a very sad fact indeed, that very few people seem to have any knowledge of history at all – beyond that which they themselves have lived through.

1.45   To make the point, let's look at Exodus 40.39, "and the Lord instructed Moses to place the two tablets of the law in the ark of the covenant and also to post a copy of the Commandments on the temple website, www.god.org". I hope anyone reading that fictional verse would then go on to question the traditional claim that the Torah was written by Moses some 3,500 years ago. However, to anyone with even a basic knowledge of the history of the ancient civilisations of Mesopotamia and Egypt – the story of Moses is so full of errors pointing to a much later, and multiple, authorship (whilst also replete with worship of pagan gods and material copied from other myths and pagan beliefs) as to render it entirely inappropriate for the books of the Torah to co-habit a book containing the Gospels.

1.46 Amazingly, the Torah and other parts of the Old Testament state quite plainly (even in English translations), in many places, information that points to the true origin of the Israelite "God". Much more surprising information is obscured in translations of Hebrew into English and by translations of the early Greek translation of the Hebrew texts in the Septuagint and subsequent translations of Masoretic and Greek texts into English.

1.47 Why have I written this book? Because I have found my voyage of discovery so exciting and so revealing – many old questions, that have lain unanswered in a dusty corner of my mind for many decades, have now been ticked off. Such as, was mankind created by God?

1.48 More seriously, I have written this book for three reasons:- firstly, to me, understanding why we exist, whether God exists, where we came from and what continuing existence we might have after we die are the most engaging and important issues of all. Secondly, the discipline of writing forced me to research and evaluate carefully what I found – and the journey has been inspiring and liberating. Thirdly, as my conclusions are exhilarating but I suspect are known only to a very few – I felt it is incumbent upon me to share the good news.

1.49 I am always surprised when I meet someone who says they don't know and don't care about God, the afterlife and such matters. I do not subscribe to dogma or to blind faith – I believe that therein lies great danger – and the root of widespread misunderstandings that have led to untold misery and slaughter over the centuries – because many people believe their adopted view is sacred and all others are sinful. This insight also explains the title of this work.

1.50 Please read and enjoy. If you find certain statements offensive, I apologize, none are intended to be. If you disagree with certain points, which is most likely, I am interested in evidence of alternative explanations. There are maybe a thousand points raised herein which conflict with, let's say, conventional Christian beliefs – for all of which I have considered whether the evidence I have uncovered can be found wanting. I am sure you will agree, the most important issue is to know the Truth. Any and all comments are most welcome – please write me, referencing the

PART ONE: GOD, ENKI, RA/MARDUK & YAHWEH

paragraph numbering herein which is designed to facilitate feedback, at truthmakesyoufree@icloud.com and I will endeavour to respond.

CHALLENGING ASPECTS OF CONVENTIONAL CHRISTIANITY

2

The Universe – spontaneous or a deliberate creation

2.1 From an early age, I pondered about the sheer scale and wild beauty of the universe. Could it all be happenstance or was a supreme intelligence behind the design.

2.2 Over the past decade, the answer seems to have become crystal clear, as humanity understands the behaviour of matter and the evolution of our universe. An erudite primer by Martin Rees, eloquently explains the vital importance of six fundamental mathematical constants which have determined the fact that our universe has evolved and the ability of matter to form stars and planets throughout our universe.

2.3 A gentle warning, this first chapter contains some basic science but please do not be put off – it is only the first ten pages and you will find it highly illuminating.

2.4 Lets take three examples, firstly the value of Gravity (N) is 10^{36} times more feeble than the electrical force attracting and repelling protons and electrons. This is a mind-numbing ratio contrasting the relative power of these two fundamental forces. If the force of gravity is 1, then the electrical force attracting and repelling protons and electrons within an atom is 1,000,000,000,000,000,000,000,000,000,000,000,000 times greater. But, because gravity always exerts an attracting force it affects objects of increasing mass disproportionately. Because gravity is so weak, a typical star has to be extremely massive for gravity to contain and crush the structures of the atoms within it, only such massive structures can generate the pressure required to crush atoms and trigger atomic fusion reaction – giving birth to a star. If gravity was weaker, say only 10^{30} weaker than electrical forces, objects would be overwhelmed by gravity at a much smaller scale. Only a billionth of such atoms would be required to form a star – in effect, a star can be defined as a gravitationally bound fusion reactor. Not only would stars be much smaller (closer to the size of Earth rather than the size of our Sun) but they would have dramatically shorter lives – 10,000 years rather than around 10 billion years. Accordingly, there would be no time for any orbiting material to coalesce into planets and certainly no time for terraforming to create an environment to support even the first rudimentary forms of life – let alone the few billion years required to evolve complex ecosystems to support intelligent beings.

2.5 As a second example, the density parameter of the universe, Ω (omega), had to be very finely tuned to initiate the expansion of the universe at a rate which almost exactly balanced the decelerating tendency of gravity. At one second after the Big Bang, Ω would have had to have differed from unity (1) by no more than one part in a million billion, (10^{15}), otherwise the universe would not still be expanding today, 13.82 billion years later.

2.6 And thirdly, the measure of nuclear efficiency, ε for epsilon, has a value of 0.007%. The value of Epsilon is the proportion of the energy contained in a hydrogen atom which is released when a fusion reaction occurs converting hydrogen to helium. Further fusion reactions, creating heavier elements, release only an additional 0.001% of the total energy for all the transmutations up to iron. If ε had a value of 0.006%, a proton could not be bonded to a neutron and deuterium would not be stable. This would block off the route to forming helium – leaving the universe comprised entirely of hydrogen – there would be no other elements: hydrogen could not fuse into helium and the stars would never have ignited and would never have made any heavier elements. There would be no carbon, no oxygen, etc.. If nuclear efficiency had been less, at say 0.008%, all protons would have fused in the big bang, preventing even hydrogen from being formed and the universe would consist only of radiation – no physical matter would exist. The sensitivity of the 0.007% value is even greater when measuring the creation of carbon and thence oxygen. Carbon is formed via an intermediate stage where beryllium combines three helium nuclei requiring a resonance (predicted by Sir Fred Hoyle) which only occurs between 0.00686% and 0.00714% nuclear efficiency – outside this narrow range no carbon, and subsequently, no oxygen could be produced.

2.7 Whilst the references above are to purely secular reference work, an openly religious writer has also focused on this vitally important issue – Hugh Ross, in his book 'Creation & Time'. On page 132, Ross states that by October 1993, "25 different characteristics of the universe were recognised as precisely fixed. If they were different by only slight amounts, the differences would spell the end of the existence of any conceivable life. To this list of 25 can be added 38 characteristics of our galaxy and solar system that likewise must fall within narrowly defined ranges for life of any kind to exist. Three of the characteristics of the universe must be defined to a precision of one part in 10^{37} or better – that's supernatural."!!

2.8 My understanding of physics is challenged by most of these characteristics – but I like the comments following the explanation of the "Fine Structure Constant":

Where e is the elementary charge, ℏ is the reduced Planck's constant, c is the speed of light in a vacuum, and ε0 is the permittivity of free space. The fine structure constant is fixed to the strength of the electromagnetic force. At low energies, α ≈ 1/137, whereas at the scale of the Z boson, about 90 GeV, one measures α ≈ 1/127. There is no accepted theory explaining the value of α – Richard Feynman elaborates:

There is a most profound and beautiful question associated with the observed coupling constant, e – the amplitude for a real electron to emit or absorb a real photon. It is a simple number that has been experimentally determined to be close to 0.08542455. (My physicist friends won't recognize this number, because they like to remember it as the inverse of its square: about 137.03597 with about an uncertainty of about 2 in the last decimal place.) It has been a mystery ever since it was discovered more than fifty years ago, and all good theoretical physicists put this number up on their wall and worry about it. Immediately you would like to know where this number for a coupling comes from: is it related to pi or perhaps to the base of natural logarithms? Nobody knows. It's one of the greatest damn mysteries of physics: a magic number that comes to us with no understanding by man. You might say the "hand of God" wrote that number, and "we don't know how He pushed his pencil." We know what kind of a dance to do experimentally to measure this number very accurately, but we don't know what kind of dance to do on the computer to make this number come out, without

$$\alpha = \frac{e^2}{\hbar c \, 4\pi\varepsilon_0} \approx \frac{1}{137.03599908},$$

putting it in secretly!

2.9 One is left with the feeling that someone set the dials very precisely to fix the physical laws governing our universe, rather like setting the dials for delicates on a galactic sized washing machine!!

2.10 Moreover, these physical laws appear to be all pervasive — fixed throughout the universe and throughout its life. These laws have enabled us to understand the chemistry from the point one millionth of a second after the Big Bang, to the end of the period of 'Inflation' when the universe had grown to the size of a golf ball containing all the energy of the universe. After around 3 seconds, protons and neutrons started to come together to form the nuclei of simple elements: hydrogen, helium and lithium. But, it took another 300,000 years for electrons to be captured into orbits around these nuclei to form stable atoms. During this time the initial bright glow from the Big Bang grew dim and the universe went dark. The dark ages lasted until the first stars evolved, igniting when the universe was about 200 million years old, as gravity caused the density of the cores of the new stars to rise and pressure caused the hydrogen to undergo fusion reaction creating helium. These first stars contained only hydrogen and some helium, and by searching the outer visible limits of the universe (13 billion light years back) we have recently identified a few strong candidates which might have been amongst the 'first stars'.

2.11 Our level of understanding has enabled scientists to develop software modelling which very accurately predicts the energy of the Big Bang evolving from radiation into matter, and gravity leading to the formation of different types of stars, the cycle of aged stars going supernova to spew out increasingly heavy elements until the current crop of young stars contains the spectrographic analysis we can observe, whilst stars form clusters of different types of galaxies and the general distribution of galaxies throughout the universe to closely resemble what we can observe today.

2.12 One amazingly useful discovery has been spectrographic analysis of starlight which provides us with detailed information on each star including the composition of elements and compounds it was made of when the light was emitted. Starlight visible to the naked eye represents only a tiny fraction of the electromagnetic spectrum of radiation emitted constantly by each star – ranked by increasing wavelength, we can capture gamma rays, x-rays, ultraviolet, visible light, infrared, microwave and radio waves. Approaching fusion temperature in a star, many atoms lose one or more of their electrons, such damaged atoms are referred to as 'ions'. The presence and distribution of different ions tells us about the temperature of the star. Each different type of atom or ion emits light waves at a combination of wavelengths, recorded as emission lines, that are unique – thereby enabling precise identification. Once astronomers have determined which ions are present in a star, we know what elements are there. We also know the temperature of that star because each type of ion is found only in a certain temperature range.

2.13　Our understanding of the early universe has been transformed by the identification of sub-atomic particles from studying collisions in the super-colliders – such as the Large Hadron Collider of CERN. This work has provided the explanation of how the universe we see around us formed, although not yet what sparked it into existence. The detail is breath taking – by the time our universe was 1 second old, the composition of matter had gone through six epochs and the initial sphere of the observable universe was 10 light years in diameter. As it takes 8.3 seconds for sunlight to reach us, to expand to 10 light years diameter in just one second is fairly dramatic.

2.14　Next, during a period from when our universe was 10 seconds old up to c17 minutes old, the universe cooled sufficiently for protons and neutrons to bind into primordial atomic nuclei – overwhelmingly hydrogen with small amounts of deuterium, helium and lithium. By the end of this period our universe occupied a sphere 300 light years in diameter.

2.15　Then over a period of 370,000 years, gradual cooling allowed electrons to combine with atomic nuclei to form the first atoms and photons to become transparent – so the lights go out, marking, what in cosmological terms is called, the Dark Ages. The imprint of this stage marks when these protons originated the cosmic microwave background radiation detected recently and mapped by satellites giving us the CMB image. By this age the universe was a sphere 42 million light years diameter.

2.16　The formation of atoms enabled the force of gravity to exploit tiny differences in the original distribution of matter leading to local concentrations which formed into stars. Around the time the universe reached 150 million years of age, these concentrations of atoms begun to attain sufficient mass for the force exerted by gravity to ignite fusion reactions – bringing light back to the universe.

2.17　Local clusters of stars formed the first galaxies but these emitted intense ultraviolet radiation that destroyed most of the remaining hydrogen atoms by knocking out their electrons (ionizing them), making it difficult for this gas to cool and for gravity to continue to form new stars. As a consequence, the process of galaxy formation ground to a halt and no new galaxies were able to form for the next billion years or so.

2.18　The hiatus in star formation came to an end when the clumps of dark matter into which the ionized gas had settled became so massive that even ionized hydrogen gas was able to cool down. This period of reionization allowed galaxy formation to resume, leading to spectacular bright galaxies; one of which is our Milky Way. Our star, the Sun, formed when the universe was around 8 billion years old.

2.19　Astronomers continue to hunt for first generation galaxies, which are expected to share significant differences compared with second generation galaxies as they had formed when the density of the universe was far higher.

2.20　So, how long is our universe designed to last? Its duration appears to be determined by the balance of forces between its initial expansionary momentum and gravity, with the critical factor being density. At the critical density, the geometry of the universe will be "flat", if the density is greater than the critical level then the geometry of our universe would be "closed", like a giant sphere and travel along a straight line would eventually return to the origin. If the actual density were lower than the critical density then the geometry would be "open" resembling a saddle. Amazingly, despite the fact that the observable density comprising matter as we know it is far below the critical density, dark matter and dark energy (two place names) make up the difference and our hypothesis explaining 'Inflation" (the first millionth of a second of our existence whence our universe expanded to the size of a golf ball) requires a flat geometry, i.e. that the actual density is at the critical density.

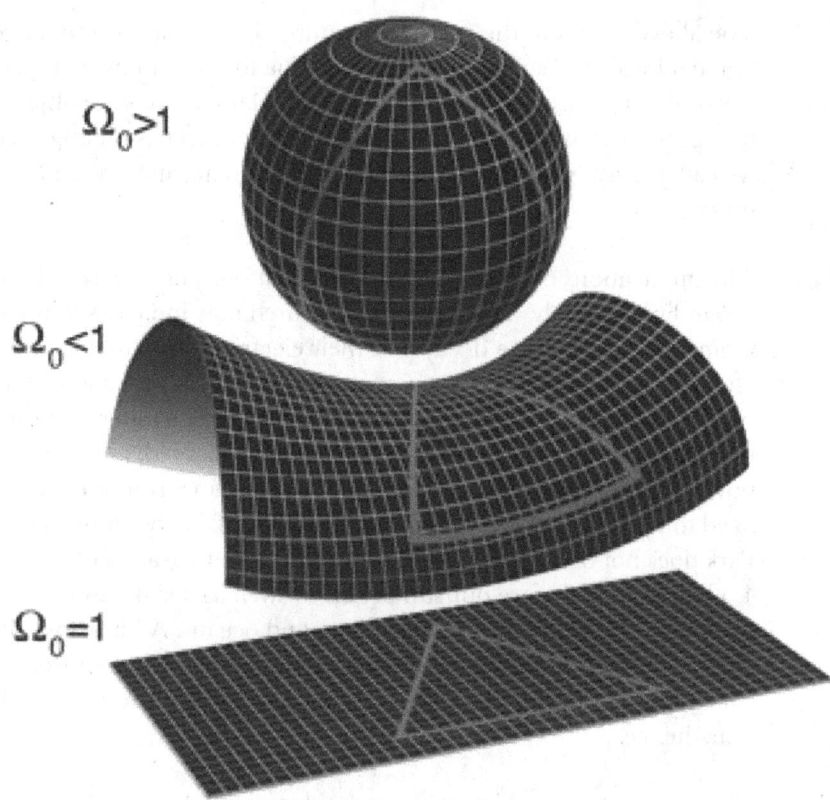

Closed universe (top), open universe (middle), and flat universe (bottom). NASA

2.21   Stunningly, measurements from the Wilkinson Microwave Anisotropy Probe (WMAP) have shown the observable universe, including dark energy and dark matter, to have a density very close to the critical density (within a 0.4% margin of error). Of course, the whole universe may be greater than the observable universe. But, we have recorded observations exceeding 13 billion light years distant, which is getting very close to the 13.82 billion year age of the universe of which we are now very confident. One big proviso to this is that whilst the atomic matter we understand may no travel faster than light, dark energy and dark matter may not be subject to this limitation and therefore the universe may have expanded to a greater size.

2.22   This flat geometry has also been validated by measurements of galactic scale triangles – whose angles sum to 180° – whereas triangles on a curved surface would sum to more than or less than 180°.

2.23 The above relates to the overall curvature of space across the universe, but at a local level space-time is curved due to the existence of mass. According to Einstein's theory of general relativity, massive objects warp the space-time around them, and the effect a warp has on objects is what we call gravity. So, locally, space-time is curved around every object with mass.

2.24 The implications of a flat geometry are that our universe could go on expanding infinitely, although some research now indicates that atoms themselves are likely to decay and their electrical structures crumble after about 50 billion years – if so, we have roughly 36 billion years left. However, before we relax too much, we should remember that our Earth, based on radiometric analysis, is 4.54 billion years old, and our star is now more than half way through its total lifespan – so eventually we will need to move elsewhere. If the next eruption of Yellowstone National Park does not obliterate us first, we will need to migrate within the next 4.5 billion years before our sun begins to swell as it starts to run out of hydrogen – vaporising our atmosphere and oceans. A bit before that we also face some turbulence when our galaxy collides with Andromeda – a galaxy roughly 3 times the mass of our Milky Way – some 3.75 billion years hence.

2.25 The precision with which so many fundamental physical characteristics were fixed to enable evolution to unfold a life-sustaining universe is breath-taking. Here lies the true awesome wonder of the Godhead!

2.26 Biology also reveals what seems to be the work of a supreme intelligence – consider DNA. This stupendously compact encyclopaedia of life form creation carries detailed instructions that enable a human to grow from a single cell to around a 100 trillion cell creature with thousands of specialised cells, all working in harmony to perform as a human. As well as being self-replicating, DNA has self-correcting enzymes which travel up and down the string constantly undertaking checking and repair of errors. The variety of life forms reflects the variety and evolution of DNA generating each variant of life form. Whilst not a biologist myself, even a basic understanding of DNA indicates that it is not a chance creation. Intriguingly, there is evidence that the ancient Sumerian civilisation understood something of DNA – their sign for a doctor, still used today, being two intertwined serpents (two wise persons) uncannily suggestive of the double helix design of DNA. We shall take a closer look at DNA in the next chapter.

2.27 But if a supreme intelligence, a sentient life form, aka God, created the universe (not "heaven and earth" – another common misunderstanding, see chapter 8) – in what form does God exist? I never bought the common view that God resembles an elderly Caucasian male with a long flowing beard. This conceptual expression of God presumably stemming from the statement in Genesis asserting that God made Man in His own image (which we shall also revisit later in section 8). My childhood concept of God envisioned an all-pervasive force that we could not hope to understand – and, to me, electricity was a suitable candidate. Actually, it seemed for many years to be a very good candidate – go check out what we really understand about electricity ! Nowadays, if pushed, I would nominate Dark Energy as the most likely candidate for the power we call God – comprising 68.3% of the energy in our universe, Dark Energy is omnipresent and currently beyond our ability to identify or contain.

2.28 Our knowledge of Dark Energy remains rather limited but much has been revealed by the data collected by the ESA Planck Space Telescope. Over several years, this collected an extremely detailed map of the Cosmic Microwave Background imprinted across our universe when it was only 0.38 million years old. Planck also enabled a record of emissions experienced over the subsequent 13.82 billion year life of our universe – as we look further away so we look further back in time. The data revealed rather surprising information – for much of its early life there seems to be little or no evidence of Dark Energy in our universe.

2.29 The emergence of Dark Energy might be linked to the gradual cooling of the universe – from 2700°C at the time of the CMB event to only 2.7°C above absolute zero today. Around 7.5 billion years ago, the proportion of Dark Energy appears to have grown to a critical level and led to a sudden acceleration in the rate of expansion of our universe. Dark Energy is now estimated to account for 68.3% of the mass energy in our universe, whilst Dark Matter (thought to be dust in interstellar space) accounts for 26.8% and Observable Matter (everything we can see) only 4.9%. Dark Energy seems to counter the force of gravity and its effect of accelerating the rate of expansion of our universe has serious implications for humanities desire to spread out and eventually make contact with other intelligent species. Latest estimates place the rate of expansion at 74.3 (+/-2.1) kilometres per second per megaparsec – considerably greater than the speed of light. Unless Scotty can engineer a way to increase warp speed by a factor of 10, we may never reach another galaxy.

2.30 The most supreme intelligence that triggered the creation of our universe and defined the parameters which governed its evolution to permit intelligent life to thrive is utterly awesome.

2.31 For me, the most humbling aspect is to learn that our universe is really all about radiation and only one obscure type of radiation transforms a tiny proportion of energy into matter – and that matter forms the environment we exist in.

THE UNIVERSE – SPONTANEOUS OR A DELIBERATE CREATION

3

Life – what did God create?

3.1 The Abrahamic faiths teach that God created Man. The well-known passage in Genesis purports that "the gods (plural) created man in their (plural) image". Questions about the odd wording are always brushed aside. However, in its literal sense we shall find that this may indeed reflect the truth – but certainly not in the way taught by the church.

3.2 How can I make such an outlandish claim? We are taught to believe Man is different to other animals – because ? Is it not obvious? We humans can think, we can talk, we have memories, we have emotions, we are intelligent! Well, actually, so are many other animals – these are by no means unique traits. Elephants, with brains four times the capacity of humans, have been found to have extraordinary memories and also to clearly show a range of emotions. Even lowly mice have been found to use a larger range of sounds to communicate between themselves than humans do. The DNA of a pig is 96% the same as a human, whilst human DNA can itself differ by up to 1% within our species.

3.3 How is mankind unique? Humans do not have the biggest brains, we do not have the best eyesight, nor the best sense of smell, nor the best hearing. Humans cannot run the fastest, are not the strongest, or toughest (e.g. most temperature tolerant), do not live the longest and cannot even fly (without mechanical support). So, why are humans so special?

3.4 Surprisingly, the key differentiator is that humans cook! All other animals devote almost their entire lives to the eating and digestion of food.

Herbivores chew cellulose almost continuously whilst carnivores have to spend time hunting and then chewing raw meat which they digest during long periods of sleep. Humanity discovered cooking and our species was transformed. The origin of cooking was most likely from the discovery of animals burned in forest fires that had ignited by lightening. Cooked meat can be eaten rapidly and digested very efficiently – providing a hugely enhanced diet for a fraction of the time devoted to consuming raw meat. This set humanity on the trail to civilisation.

3.5 When we look for historical references to the origin of human cooking we find something quite intriguing. The Sumerian records (from translations of cuneiform tablets excavated from Iraq) tell of a time when men, unclothed, ate raw food, in the field, with their hands. This is also depicted in ancient Egyptian reliefs. Sumerian records also tell of the ingredients and cooking recipes demanded by specific gods. But when we read Genesis, there is no reference to God teaching Man to cook. In Genesis, El Elyon does help Adam and Eve to make clothes but there is no mention of cooking. Much later, Yahweh finds the Israelites eating cooked food and specifies how he would like his food prepared (providing detailed butchery instructions) and specifying how his bread should be baked (without yeast).

3.6 So, let's get back to what makes humans special. Some believe, including myself, that our human distinction is derived from hosting some spiritual force, a spirit that is of God. But, as we shall see, that does not mean God created us – all the evidence suggests we existed, and evolved, long before any spirit entered us. So, it seems more likely that God or the gods 'found' humanity and decided we had potential.

3.7 In this chapter we shall explore how life works and why it seems most probable that God designed life but not humanity. That will shock many people but it is similar to our discovery in the previous chapter that, yes, God designed the complex ways that atoms behave in our universe – but God certainly did not create Earth. Our planet was simply an inevitable product of the machinery God put in motion. Nor is Earth likely to be anything like unique, it is probable that there are uncounted millions of Earth like planets. Nor is Earth particularly stable or long lasting. Human life on Earth has only been possible for our species for a small fraction of Earth's 4543 million year existence and it could become uninhabitable again very suddenly – from a large meteor impact or from the gigantic magma chamber beneath Yellowstone National Park erupting once again.

3.8   Biology is a way of structuring matter and controlling flows of energy at a molecular scale by slotting each atom into its specified place. Until Charles Darwin developed the theory of evolution in 1875, we had assumed that the vast array of life forms on our planet had been individually created by God. Evolution explains how life forms will adapt to changing environments, those with attributes most suited to particular climatic conditions and food resources will flourish whilst those less well suited will struggle – summed up as the survival of the fittest.

3.9   Archaeological and genetic evidence indicates humans first begun to cross pollinate wild cereals and pulses around 9000BC and first begun selective breeding to domesticate goats and sheep around 8000BC. Chinese voyages of discovery in the 1420's spread chickens around the world whilst, starting a century later, the 'Columbian exchange' begun large scale mixing together the fauna and flora of Eurasia and the Americas.

3.10   In the past few decades, truly staggering knowledge of how life works, how it may be modified and even created from scratch from its constituent materials has been uncovered. DNA (deoxyribonucleic acid) is located in the cell nucleus of virtually every cell of our bodies and almost every other life form on Earth. DNA comprises a twisted double helix of information containing about 3 billion base pairs storing code comprising four chemicals:- adenine (A), guanine (G), cytosine (C), and thymine (T). Each base pair is linked to a sugar molecule and a phosphate molecule – with the base pair forming a step and the sugar and phosphate forming something like the sides of a ladder – the sequence of these steps (nucleotides) forms the information to build and maintain the specific life form. Each cell in a human contains an exact copy of its DNA. DNA operates a host of mechanisms, using a range of tailored enzymes to check for uniformity and repair any transcription errors when copying.

3.11   Differences in DNA between different humans is less than 1%. Studies have found amazing degrees of similarity between humans and other species – chimpanzees are closest, sharing 96% DNA in common with humans. The Abyssinian domestic cat shares 90%; mice share 85%; cows share 80%; zebrafish share 70%; chickens and fruit flies share 60% and even the banana tree, without any of what we term 'vital organs', shares about 55% DNA with humans!! The shared genetic material found in the zebrafish is so great that 84% of all human genetic diseases can be studied in zebrafish!!

3.12   In the 1950's we discovered that genes, the instruction sets used to build molecules of proteins, were written on long strands of DNA – resembling stock prices on an old fashioned ticker-tape. We learned how each gene specialised in using combinations of amino-acids in a specified sequence to make a protein which was then used by DNA to make specified parts of an organ in a life form.

3.13   By the 1970's, we started to transfer traits from organisms in which they had evolved to organisms we wanted to exhibit such traits – simply by cutting and pasting sections of the ticker-tape! Thus was born the bio-technology industry.

3.14   In the 1980's we designed machines that could synthesise DNA letter by letter, which were soon used to create wholly new gene sequences, not found in nature, building cells which work in whole new ways – effectively reprogramming cells.

3.15   Soon after 2000, academic research established that biology, like computing, is based on digital code – and that cells could be engineered in the same way that electrical circuits and software codes are. An amazing advance flowed from the discovery in 2007 of a cellular defence enzyme, named CRISPR-cas9, which cuts up and destroys any foreign DNA that invades a cell. "CRISPR" stands for "clusters of regularly inter-spaced short palindromic repeats". It is a specialized region of DNA with two distinct characteristics: the presence of nucleotide repeats and spacers. Repeated sequences of nucleotides — the building blocks of DNA — are distributed throughout a CRISPR region. Spacers are bits of DNA that are interspersed among these repeated sequences.

3.16   The "cas9" protein is an enzyme which acts as a pair of scissors, cutting up the attacking DNA and absorbing the alien spacers to serve as a memory bank to identify and fight off similar attacks in the future. Once a spacer is incorporated and the virus attacks again, a portion of the CRISPR is transcribed and processed into CRISPR RNA, or "crRNA". The nucleotide sequence of the CRISPR acts as a template to produce a complementary sequence of single-stranded RNA. The cas9 protein typically binds to two RNA molecules: crRNA and another called tracrRNA (or "trans-activating crRNA"). The two then guide cas9 to the target site where it will make its cut.

3.17 Genes encode a series of messages and instructions within their DNA sequences. Gene editing involves changing those sequences, thereby changing the messages. This can be done by inserting a cut or break in the DNA and tricking a cell's natural DNA repair mechanisms into introducing the changes wanted. CRISPR-Cas9 has proved to be a very efficient mechanism to do so.

3.18 In 2012, two pivotal research papers were published which transformed CRISPR-Cas9 into a simple, programmable gene-editing tool. These studies concluded that Cas9 could be directed to cut any region of DNA. This could be done by simply changing the nucleotide sequence of crRNA, which binds to a complementary DNA target. One team simplified the process by fusing crRNA and tracrRNA to create a single "guide RNA". Thus, gene editing requires only two components: a guide RNA and the Cas9 protein.

3.19 In 2013, the first reports of using CRISPR-Cas9 to edit human cells in an experimental setting were published by researchers from MIT and Harvard. Studies using models of human disease have demonstrated that the technology can be effective in correcting genetic defects such as cystic fibrosis and cataracts. Thus CRISPR may be applied clinically to cure disease.

3.20 On 4 March 2020, The Guardian reported that CRISPR-Cas9 had been used inside a person's body for the first time to operate directly on DNA to treat a disease. The case involved a patient with an inherited form of blindness and was undertaken at the Casey Eye Institute at Oregon Health & Science University in Portland. The condition, Leber congenital amaurosis, is caused by a gene mutation that keeps the body from making a protein needed to convert light into signals to the brain. Treatment cannot use standard gene therapy – supplying a replacement gene – because the one needed is too big to fit inside the disabled viruses that are used to ferry it into cells. So the new treatment aims to edit or delete the mutation by making two cuts on either side of it. The hope is that the ends of DNA will reconnect and allow the gene to work as it should. The surgery entails dripping three drops of fluid containing the gene editing machinery through a tube the width of a hair to just beneath the retina, the lining at the back of the eye that contains the light-sensing cells. Dr Eric Pierce at Massachusetts Eye and Ear noted that once the cell is edited, it's permanent and that cell will persist – hopefully for the life of the patient because these cells don't divide. Doctors think they need to fix between one-tenth and one-third of the cells to restore vision. In animal tests, scientists were able to correct half of the cells with the treatment.

3.21   Charles Albright, Chief Scientific Officer at Editas Medicine, the company developing the treatment for Leber congenital amaurosis jointly with Allergan, said it could open up a whole new set of medicines to go in and change your DNA. Doctors first tried in-the-body gene editing in 2017 for a different inherited disease using a tool known as zinc fingers. Many scientists believe CRISPR-Cas9 is a much better tool for locating and cutting DNA at a specific spot.

3.22   Meanwhile CRISPR-Cas9 has also being applied to engineer probiotic cultures to vaccinate products such as yogurt; to re-engineer seeds to improve crop yields, drought tolerance and nutritional properties.

3.23   Another interesting application is the creation of gene drives – genetic modification introduced to a population with the intention of being passed from generation to generation. One application has been to enhance sterility amongst female Anopheles mosquitoes to suppress malaria.

3.24   In the past decade, synthetic biology was born. Essentially biology is the manufacture of proteins which then carry out all the basic functions of life – breathing, digesting food, etc.. Each protein is made from 20 amino acids strung together in a chain. The shape these chains fold into to fulfil different functions are both complex and unpredictable – but appear to be determined by the sequence of the amino acids. The gene for a given protein is simply a section of the DNA, a sequence of the 64 three letter combinations that can be made from the four bases (adenine, cytosine, thymine and guanine – usually referred to as simply A, C, T & G). These 64 combinations are called codons and each has a specific amino acid meaning. Each gene is an algorithm, a set of sequential rules to make a protein. The cell employs codon-recognising, amino-acid-carrying molecules called trnas and a mechanism called a ribosome which provides a place for those trnas to interact with a copy of the gene. The act of reading the gene, codon by codon, is the act of creating the protein, amino acid by amino acid.

3.25 CRISPR-cas9 opened up the potential to build new enzymes which will in turn create new proteins.

3.26 We have identified the software code by which cells turn genes on and off. Only when a gene is on, or "expressed", will a cell make the protein described by that gene's ticker-tape sequence. When it is turned off, or "repressed", the protein's production stops. Because proteins are the molecules that carry out almost all the tasks that go on in a cell, which genes are expressed and when – is fundamental to how cells work. When it executes an algorithm this way, biology looks like computer science. But biology does not deal with information the way humans do. In human programs, the logic and the machinery that acts on it are kept separate. Computer users can change a program in blithe ignorance of the physical principles and peculiarities built into the hardware that it runs on. But life does not make any such distinction. Biological processing is simply molecules interacting—the way that trnas stick to codons as if to velcro, the way the shape of the ribosome forces amino-acids together, and so on. From the simple gene-to-protein translation of the ribosome to the extraordinary synchronised symphony which turns a fertilised egg into a whole human, biological information and its implementation are all but inseparable. Life runs not on software and hardware, but in allware.

3.27 It has been estimated that nature has developed around 5m proteins but most remain unexplored. Nor is it clear to us yet what each of those we have studied actually do. Thus the potential diversity of alien life is virtually unlimited. Even the simplest bacterium contains proteins with jobs that scientists cannot identify—but which the bacterium clearly considers vital because, if the genes producing those proteins are removed, it dies. If many specific functions are still hazy, the cumulative capability of all the things that natural proteins can do is well known: it is the living world. The action of proteins creates all the diverse lifeforms we see around us – from coral reefs to mosquitoes and from trees to humans.

3.28 Now, technology enables new proteins to be designed at will. Most proteins contain 66 links, with 20 different amino-acid possibilities for each of the links in the chain, so that, in principle, there are 20^{66} potential proteins. That is roughly the same as the number of subatomic particles in the visible universe – to write out such a number would require more than two lines in this booklet. This paragraph is worth reading again.

3.29 Initially, research teams tried to modify existing organisms. One target was E-coli – a laboratory made version was designed with a radically reduced genetic code. Nearly all life, from jellyfish to humans, uses 64 codons. Codons are the three letter 'words' listing the amino acids required to make a specified protein. But many seem to be duplications – 61 codons make only 20 different natural amino acids, which can be strung together like beads on a string to build any protein in nature. Three more codons act as stop signs: they tell the cell when the protein being created is complete. The Cambridge team set out to redesign the E coli genome by removing some of its superfluous codons. Working on a computer, the scientists went through the bug's DNA. Whenever they came across TCG, a codon that makes an amino acid called serine, they rewrote it as AGC, which does the same job. They replaced two more codons in a similar way.

3.30 After 18,000 edits, every occurrence of the three codons had been removed from the bug's genome. The redesigned genetic code was then chemically synthesised and, piece by piece, added to E coli where it replaced the organism's natural genome. The result, known as Syn61, is a little longer than natural E coli and grows more slowly, but survives nonetheless. Such synthetic life forms bring benefits for the biopharma industry – whereas natural E coli is used to make insulin and other medical compounds for cancer, multiple sclerosis and eye diseases – entire production runs can be spoiled when bacterial cultures are contaminated by viruses. Syn61 has novel defences, its different DNA making it virus resistant. Syn61 proved life can exist with a restricted genetic code and paved the way for organisms whose biological machinery is commandeered to make drugs and useful materials, or to add new features such as virus resistance.

3.31 Plus there is another bonus – the freed up codons can be re-purposed to make amino acids that do not occur naturally in DNA to manufacture new designer enzymes and proteins. Nature only uses 20 amino acids in its proteins. But there are hundreds of others that could be created – these would confer interesting new properties. Another synthetic genome has been created, Sc2.0, for which the original tag codon can be re-purposed to create an artificial trna molecule which recognises the tag codon and then creates a new amino acid that nature has never used before – at least on planet Earth. Given that the 20 amino acids naturally occurring on Earth are created by no less than 61 codons, it appears there is scope to introduce up to 41 new amino acids in each new synthetic life form. Given the amazing diversity of life on this planet already, this suggests the scope for diversification is staggering.

3.32 At a time when antibiotics are being defeated by viruses in ever shortening timeframes, this opens up the potential of confronting viruses with genetic codes they have never seen before – making such cells immune. This sort of recoding could provide fermentation tanks that never get contaminated by infections and antibody-producing cell lines that could not harbour viruses. Some have suggested changes to codons so radical that one creates synthetic biology which becomes a separate creation, parallel biospheres based on the original but no longer in contact with it, populated by creatures which neither infect nor are infected. Maybe, one day we use such techniques to create such a biology to colonise Mars.

3.33 Another mind boggling possibility was published in January 2019 in Science by Stephen Benner of the Foundation for Applied Molecular Evolution in Florida and his colleagues. They have created double helices in which the four existing bases, a, t, c and g, are supplemented by z, p, s and b. This hachimoji ("eight letters") DNA offers much denser data storage than evolution has had at its disposal for the past 4bn years. With eight letters to play with, for example, you could recode the genome to use doublets, rather than triplets, as codons – vastly increasing the potential range of amino acids and proteins that might be designed for use within a single life form.

3.34 The potential glimpsed by these technologies is almost beyond comprehension. But is there really much impact so far? Yes, by 2017 it was estimated that the value of products manufactured by genetically engineered life forms accounted for 2% of US GDP – some US$388 billion!! This amount comprised broadly equal contributions from pharmaceuticals, crop seeds and industrial products such as food additives, fragrances and biofuels. Many players now offer bio engineering services – e.g. how to make an organism more productive. Tim Fell, the boss of Synthace, a synthetic-biology software company in London, reported that in one project his company bio-engineered a 200-fold increase in the rate at which bacteria produced something useful in just four weeks. Another bioengineer, Gingko, created a joint venture with Bayer, a chemicals giant, to develop microbes which will manufacture fertiliser inside a plant's root system.

3.35 Companies such as Gingko and Arzeda (a protein design company) already process customer orders involving the creation of tens of thousands of artificial DNA sequences every week. Processes are being automated to handle this – Ginkgo spent years programming computers to supervise experiments and robots to construct the artificial DNA and to find and remove the innumerable bugs with which those programs were afflicted.

3.36 Other companies are designing programming logic into protein design by for example adding conditionality or 'and' gates which is providing new, more precise, ways of knocking out cancer cells.

3.37 In October 2019, reports emerged of fresh hopes for treating people with genetic disorders by inventing a powerful new molecular tool more powerful than CRISPA-cas9 that, in principle, can correct the vast majority of mutations that cause human genetic diseases. The procedure, named "prime editing", can mend about 89% of the 75,000 or so harmful mutations known to mangle the human genome and lead to conditions such as cystic fibrosis and sickle cell anaemia. This technique improves the sometime haphazard approach of cas9 which bluntly severs the DNA helix and can lead to random insertions, deletions and other genetic detritus that can interfere with the workings of the edited cell. This is less problematic when scientists are working on cells in a dish, because those that are affected can be thrown away. However, when genome editing is used to rewrite faulty genes in people's lungs, hearts and other tissues, far more precision is needed.

3.38 Prime editing is a major enhancement in precision. Instead of just cutting the DNA helix and inserting material, Prime Editing makes a nick in one side and then inserts the new code to be inserted at the site. Another protein then triggers a cut on the other strand and the cell repairs by copying the new code into the second strand of the helix completing the edit. An article in Nature published on 21 October 2019, reports how a team corrected mutations that cause the inherited blood disorder, sickle cell anaemia. In another, they removed the four extra DNA letters in a particular gene that cause Tay-Sachs disease, a rare condition that destroys children's nerves and usually proves fatal by five years old.

3.39 The amazing new vaccines developed in record time during 2020 to combat Covid-19 have exploited these new DNA based techniques. The new vaccines are using techniques that were already under development to target specific types of cancer. Laboratory designed mRNA is being deployed to target very specific changes in human DNA to enable our immune system to trigger specially designed immune reactions to destroy Covid-19 cells.

3.40 Pharmacologists have seized on this opportunity, realizing that instead of trying to manufacture proteins with their complex irregular shapes which are designed to fit into target cells to allow drugs to exercise their purpose, they now see a much more effective route employing Prime Editing to deliver edits to our DNA to resolve a problem at source instead of trying to deal with the effects of a disease.

3.41 The greatest discovery in molecular biology, following our discovery of DNA's double-helix structure, is the realisation that the rules of shape and sequence are linked. The shape of a protein depends on the intricate way in which the chain of amino acids which it consists of is folded. This folding follows the sequence in which the different amino acids are strung together on the chain. The sequence of the amino acids is a crucial part of the genetic information stored in the DNA sequences of the cell's genome. RNA is the key mechanism by which the stored data in DNA is activated – the sequence of amino acids determines the shape created which in turn is critical to performing its purpose. The code stored in DNA is copied into RNA and edited to form a molecule of messenger RNA, mRNA. The mRNA molecule is recognised by ribosomes carrying proteins which aided by trna's stick to the mRNA and creates a chain on amino acids as the message is read.

3.42 mRNA Covid vaccines developed by BioNTech and Moderna used this technique to enable our mRNA to use ribosomes to create new amino acids which could recognise, attack and destroy Covid-19 viruses. These companies mass produced an RNA sequence presenting the distinctive Covid spike protein and wrap them in a liposome bubble, which when injected, enters our cells. When ribosomes read the mRNA they produce the spike protein and the Covid virus is attacked. This capability, of getting cells to churn out proteins which are not described by genes pre-existing in our DNA opens up a huge range of therapeutic opportunities. Drugmakers are now moving from focusing on the shapes of proteins to studying sequence. Instead of targeting proteins that are already present, now they can target the processes which control which proteins get made in the first place, adding helpful new ones to the process and cutting out production of harmful proteins.

3.43   By Spring 2021, there were already mRNA based drugs in clinical trials for the treatment of cancer, heart disease and numerous inherited disorders—as well as brain diseases such as Alzheimer's and Parkinson's. BioNTech is developing vaccines to treat a wide range of cancers. Cancer cells often have specific arrays of proteins on their surfaces, including normal ones that are overexpressed and mutant forms peculiar to the development of that tumour. Comparing the genes expressed in a patient's healthy cells with those used by their tumour cells reveals which mutant proteins the cancers are producing; mRNA's for those proteins can then be incorporated into a vaccine. Produced as a result of vaccination, the new proteins can trigger a vigorous immune response the cancer previously avoided by deploying mechanisms that stop the immune system from reacting. Moderna is developing vaccines that train the immune system to recognise proteins created by common mutations in KRAS, a gene implicated in about 20% of human cancers. Moderna is also looking at vaccines against herpes, three lung viruses affecting children and Zika, a mosquito-borne virus found mainly in the tropics. Moderna is working with AstraZeneca on developing an mRNA to encourage the regrowth of blood vessels. This therapy could stimulate the growth of new cardiac blood vessels after heart attacks.

3.44   The combination of sequence and shape carried by mRNA means that the once-haphazard process of drug discovery, dependent on matching the shape of small synthetic molecules to the nooks and crannies of the proteins they targeted, can be systematised. A sequence which recognises one gene can be switched out for a sequence tailored to another. When what the operation of an mRNA drug depends on its sequence, its target and action can be modified by the click of a mouse.

3.45   Another firm, Ionis Pharmaceuticals, has been working since 1989 on a different aspect of the mRNA mechanism, namely that production of a harmful protein might be blocked if an 'antisense' mRNA could be injected. The mRNA mechanism works by being produced by DNA as a complimentary copy which when read then reproduces the original instructions. If an mRNA molecule is introduced which is an exact copy of the DNA sequence, being complementary it will stick to the original mRNA and prevent it producing the damaging protein. Obviously, this is easier said than done but Ionis got their first antisense drug approved in 2016 and seven years later had 37 antisense molecules in clinical trials for a variety of illnesses including Alzheimer's, Parkinson's disease, cystic fibrosis and Huntington's disease.

3.46 Another stunning development during 2020 was the development by DeepMind (a subsidiary of Alphabet Inc.) of software to predict the shape of newly invented proteins, i.e. proteins which do not occur naturally in Earth's biosphere. Predicting the shape of artificially designed proteins will enable us to gain some idea of how a new protein might perform and what use it might be put to. Such modelling power will dramatically change our ability to design new proteins to solve specific biological problems. Given the potential number of new proteins, 20^{66} as mentioned in paragraph 3.28 above, this opens up almost infinite potential. Eventually, we might be able to reprogram our own DNA to continuously repair and renew all our organs, we might set out to enhance the capabilities of our organs (e.g. improve our eyesight, develop self-cleaning arteries, etc.) – to make ourselves more or less immortal.

3.47 Clearly, humans have now harnessed the biology of life and are exploiting it for monetary gain. No one thinks about boundaries. Animal testing of cosmetics on animals including primates generated a very negative reaction – but where will be drawn the line for synthetic biology? For some years now, humans have been discussing the potential to use pigs to 'grow' human organs. We generally look down upon pigs, indeed many regard pigs as impure – what will an individual say if offered a lifesaving heart transplant from a pig? More importantly, the DNA of a pig and a human share 96% commonality – a pig is actually quite closely related to us. How do we know whether a pig lacks a spirit or lacks a soul? In the past some Christians did so believe, including the Cathars of the Pyrenees in medieval times.

3.48 All life on Earth uses DNA as its operating system. DNA created dinosaurs which ruled the planet for around 300 million years, whilst we Homo Sapiens Sapiens have only been around for some 175,000 years. As referred to in paragraph 3.37 above, we have so far identified around 75,000 errors which have arisen in human DNA – and have now discovered the tools which might be used to rectify these errors.

3.49 In May 2018, The New York Times reported on research by Jordi Paps of the University of Essex and Peter W.H. Holland of the University of Oxford that identified 55% of the genes in the human genome were found to have been present in the very earliest animal yet discovered – some 650 million years ago. For example, the earliest sharks used the same gene sequence to make haemoglobin as humans do – indicating a common ancestor as the source of dinosaurs, sharks and humans. Again, this points not to God creating mankind but very much to God having designed DNA.

3.50 Indeed, the biggest question might be whether DNA originated on Earth or travelled here on an asteroid? The similarity of the DNA operating all lyfeforms on our planet indicates DNA was planted here – by design or by accident. If DNA had evolved on Earth, one would expect far greater differentiation between the operating systems across Earthly lyfeforms.

3.51 In 2019 a Japanese spacecraft, the Japan Space Agency Hayabusa 2 mission, landed on the Ryugu asteroid (250m km from Earth) and retrieved samples which were returned to Earth in a sealed canister. Yasuhiro Oba of Hokkaido University emphasised the security measures deployed to ensure there was no possibility of contamination. Subsequent analysis revealed the samples contained two essential compounds used by RNA – niacin and uracil. Niacin is known as Vitamin B3, nicotinic acid. Oba reported that samples taken from two different sites on Ryugu both contained niacin and uracil. Whilst it seems unlikely that these compounds developed in situ on the sterile environment of an asteroid, the asteroid itself is probably a remnant of a planet or ejecta from a meteor impacting a planet. Thus the origin of these compounds is likely to have been from a planet on which the building blocks of life had at least started to emerge. One can speculate whether the existence of these compounds points to something similar in function to RNA or DNA having evolved elsewhere.

3.52 Previously, scientists had detected key organic compounds in carbon-rich meteorites found on Earth but the possibility of contamination on Earth left the extra-terrestrial origin of the compounds compromised. Now, we hold proof such compounds seem to naturally evolve remote from our planet.

3.53 We have even more promising samples on their way to Earth. On 24th

September 2023, the NASA mission OSIRIS-REx, is scheduled to return samples from another asteroid, Bennu. Bennu is a carbonaceous asteroid, with substantial volumes of water in its surface compounds – offering good prospects of finding carbon based compounds used by RNA. If the results confirm the presence of elements used in RNA, we may have to re-evaluate our views on the likelihood of life existing elsewhere. Bennu, with a mean diameter of 0.5km, is listed as a potentially hazardous object with the highest risk fly by currently forecast for 24 September 2182. The force of an impact by Bennu is estimated at some 80,000 times the explosive power of Hiroshima and leave an impact crater around 5km wide.

3.54 In its search extra-terrestrial life, NASA has had to develop a definition of life. Their working description is "a self-sustaining chemical system capable of Darwinian evolution". Nasa's astrobiology programme has developed a novel and broader definition of life – a definition that encapsulates life on Earth but also the possibility of "life not as we know it" – they term it "lyfe". As explained in this chapter, all life on Earth uses DNA as its operating system – despite the diversity of life on Earth, it appears that every living organism can be traced back to a common ancestor. Life on other planets may have emerged differently – therefore we need a broader definition. Stuart Bartlett at Caltech, and Michael L Wong, an astrobiologist at the University of Washington have developed a new hypothetical concept: "lyfe". They define a "lyving" organism as satisfying four criteria:

- dissipation (the ability to harness and convert free energy sources);

- autocatalysis (the ability to grow or expand exponentially);

- homeostasis (the ability to limit change internally when things change externally); and,

- learning (the ability to record, process and carry out actions based on information).

With this definition, life is just one specific instance of lyfe.

3.55 Summer 2020 has seen a number of space probes launched towards Mars to exploit the favourable celestial alignment. In Stuart Bartlett's opinion, there is a higher probability of finding lyfe on Mars than life.

No one expects to find little green men but finding any form of lyfe will transform humanity. Martian organisms may use a different molecular structure. Perhaps they use a smaller set of amino acids for proteins. Perhaps they only need a doublet genetic code, instead of a triplet like life on Earth. When the Martian rock samples are returned to Earth for analysis in 2026, humanity will be on the edge of its most shocking discovery – there are three possible outcomes, each will have a big psychological impact:

- despite the promising site, Jezero Crater, and previous evidence that Mars had a balmy climate and plentiful water – no evidence of life is detected. This will be a great disappointment but hope will remain for the future.

- evidence of DNA based life is found – many will conclude such life must have existed on Mars long before such life could have existed on Earth – life here is, in effect, a Martian colony. However, this is unlikely unless DNA based life managed to cling on below ground on Mars for around 2 billion years after that planet lost its magnetosphere, water and most of its atmosphere.

- evidence of lyfe is found – proving DNA is not the unique operating system supporting lifeforms, prompting us to ponder what diversity our galaxy might contain?

Whether or not we find evidence of lyfe on Mars, various moons of the outer planets offer promising environments – in particular Titan, Enceladus and Europa.

3.56 Some are enthusiastic to form human colonies on Mars and hope to harness local natural resources to support life. However, the most effective way to terraform a planet and at the same time evolve perfectly suited life forms for its environment would be to seed a planet with DNA. One would have to plan such a project on a non-human timescale – but maybe other species have done this? After reading this chapter, you might feel it is time for a stiff drink!!

LIFE – WHAT DID GOD CREATE?

4

The contrasting characters of Yahweh and Jesus

4.1 Jesus, by any standard, is truly exceptional. His recorded statements and sermons show a uniquely pure love towards all mankind and absolute loyalty to his "Father". His character and behaviour is that which all mankind might aspire to but quite beyond our individual attainment for even short periods. The only recorded event which might be identified as a departure from the highest standard of love shown repeatedly to all manner of sinners would be the disturbance in the Temple, when Jesus turned over the tables of some foreign exchange dealers. The character of Jesus, as described in the Bible, stands in very stark contrast to the description of the character of God as described throughout the Old Testament.

4.2 For the most part, Christians cleave to the concept of a Triune God comprising God, his Spirit and Jesus, his son – a concept that is hard to fathom. We shall examine later, where this concept originated and why it was adopted (section 17). The concept certainly troubled me, as the character of the God that created the universe is unfathomably majestic and awesome beyond our understanding whilst the character of Jesus is easier to understand but of such stunning purity that we easily understand that we are all sinners – in need of forgiveness and salvation.

4.3 But, when I look at the God of the Old Testament, particularly throughout the Torah, this God is filled with the worst character traits of humankind – full of anger, trickery, self-confessed jealousy, and with an insatiable bloodlust not only towards any of the enemies of his Chosen People, but extending to clear instructions to commit genocide against those who just happened to be living in lands regarded as having been identified for resettlement. Instances occur where the Israelites are judged not to have been ruthless enough – and "God" is angry because his instructions for genocide were not fully implemented. Really? Extraordinary events, such as the instruction (Exodus 32.17) given to Moses inner circle to rampage through the Israelites camp beside Mount Sinai, indiscriminately massacring their brothers and neighbours – in fact, those who had merely followed Aaron (Moses brother) in worshipping the golden calf, the son of the god they thought they were being led by (this is explained in section 12).

4.4 Further, the instruction by Yahweh (Numbers 31:15-18) to commit genocide against the Midianites, the Chief Priest of whom, Jethro, was Moses father in law, and whose seven daughters Moses is described as having recently lived with for 40 years – is unbelievable! The Israelite army returned having razed all the Midianite towns and brought back captive all the Midianite women and children. Yahweh then instructed all the boys should be massacred and all the women except the virgins should also be massacred – leaving 32,000 virgins to be shared out amongst the troops. The Bible is bashfully silent about the fate of Moses six sisters-in-law! This behaviour is far worse than the Prophet Mohammed (PbuH) metered out to his enemies – who were at least offered alternative options of converting to Islam or of paying the jizya tax. Even more startling is evidence that the Midianites chief deity, for whom Jethro was priest, was none other than "YHW". YHW was almost certainly the inspiration for Moses adoption of "YHWH", as the new name for god as revealed to him towards the end of his 40 years sojourn with Jethro and his seven daughters.

4.5 The recorded genocide metered out on the Midianites was not an isolated case – the 60 cities of Bashan (Deuteronomy 3:4-6) and the seven nations in Canaan (Deuteronomy 7:1-2) were also marked out for the same treatment.

4.6 Yahweh repeatedly threatened the Israelites that he would make them eat their own children – Leviticus 26:29; Deuteronomy 28:53-57; Jeremiah 19:9; Ezekiel 5:10; Lamentations 4:10 – can you imagine Jesus threatening such barbarity? Yet the Church purports that Yahweh and Jesus are two expressions of the same triune God – it baffles me that anyone accepts this.

4.7 It is also instructive to review Jesus references to the "Jewish" faith. Jesus dismisses complete chunks of Mosaic law – as in Mark 7:15-18 where he states "nothing going into a man's stomach makes him unholy ('unclean') only what comes out of his heart is unholy". This is followed by calling his disciples "dull" when they don't seem to understand and he has to repeat the point – what goes into a man's mouth goes into his stomach and later leaves him, all evil comes out from within a man's heart. Jesus states that there is no such thing as unclean foods. In Acts 10, the Lord appears in a dream instructing Peter to kill and eat any animal, then in response to Peter's refusal to eat anything unclean, the Lord says to him "do not call anything impure that God has made clean".

4.8 Jesus famously sought out those marked by Hebrew society as "unclean", sinners or worse – the leper, the lame, the tax collector, the prostitute, even the dead. In John 6:37, Jesus is quoted as saying "whoever comes to me, I will never drive away". This is in stark contrast to Yahweh, who in Leviticus 21:16-23 states:

> *"The Lord said to Moses, "Say to Aaron: 'For the generations to come, none of your descendants who has a defect may come near to offer the food of his God. No man who has any defect may come near: no man who is blind or lame, disfigured or deformed; no man with a crippled foot or hand, or who is a hunchback or a dwarf, or who has any eye defect, or who has festering or running sores or damaged testicles. No descendant of Aaron the priest who has any defect is to come near to present the food offerings to the Lord. He has a defect; he must not come near to offer the food of his God. He may eat the most holy food of his God, as well as the holy food; yet because of his defect, he must not go near the curtain or approach the altar, and so desecrate my sanctuary. I am the Lord, who makes them holy.' "*

4.9 How can we believe any physical defect renders a person ineligible to come before God? Further, how can anyone believe Yahweh and Jesus are part of the same triune God? WWJD – for me to believe that Yahweh and Jesus are part of the same Godhead, Leviticus 21 would need to say something like "and if anyone is found with any defect (insert list of ailments) then bring him into the Tent and lay him before me and I, your Holy God, shall make him whole and perfect, for I am the Lord your God" – but the Torah states the exact opposite!

4.10 When Jesus robe was touched by a woman who had 'suffered from bleeding for 12 years' and according to Leviticus was therefore unclean and committing a sin, Jesus did not rebuke her but healed her. (Matthew 9:20-22; Mark 5:25-34)

4.11 Likewise, Jesus dismisses the heavy religious rituals formulated in the Torah but confusingly also appears to confirm their observance in Matthew 23. However, Matthew 23 appears to be an aberration, maybe written in to reassure the Jewish readers to whom the gospel of Matthew was addressed. There is clear evidence, as will be examined later, in Part Three, that the Gospel of Matthew suffers from a number of, no doubt well intentioned, embellishments to promote Jesus and Church dogma.

4.12 My findings from research of the Torah clearly have implications for my understanding of Christianity and in particular OT prophesies concerning Jesus. These findings are discussed in detail in Part Three.

4.13 My brief references to what pastors refer to as "difficult passages" in the Old Testament have led me to wonder the relevance of the entire Old Testament to Christians. The stock response is of course, Jesus always referred to the Jewish God as his Father – did he? Jesus did frequently refer to God as his Father but never mentioned Yahweh, moreover it seems clear Jesus did not mean 'father' in a biological sense – I will revert to this point. An early Church leader, actually the first to assemble a series of 'books' into the very first Bible, Marcion, strongly refuted any connection between the Jewish scripture and Jesus. Indeed, after the early centuries when successive Church Councils argued about which books to include or exclude from biblical canon, the Roman Catholic Church relegated the entire Old Testament and focused its services and preaching on the books of the New Testament. The Catholic leadership clearly understood something was seriously wrong with the contents of the bible – as the laity were generally prohibited from owning or reading even part of the Bible until surprisingly recently. This historical background is explored in greater detail in Part Four.

4.14 I can almost hear readers exclaim, hold on – there are supposed to be many, even hundreds, of prophesies about Jesus in the Old Testament – therefore it must be part of the whole message from God? Further on, we shall look closely at what are regarded as the most powerful prophesies.

4.15 We shall also consider the extent to which current bibles accurately and completely reflect Jesus teaching. We know the church campaigned ruthlessly for many centuries to destroy any texts it felt contradicted what it had determined as dogma. Gradually we have discovered the titles of over a hundred 1st Century Christian texts of which all copies had been believed to be destroyed. Innumerable people were killed merely because they possessed a proscribed book, something deemed heretical and a threat to the purity of church dogma. Whilst difficult, as almost all records were successfully destroyed, some remaining texts point to startling differences between early Christian beliefs and Catholic dogma which has passed, largely intact, to all the Protestant denominations. To capture your interest, consider the disciples who toured the then extant provinces of Judah, Samaria and Galilee with Jesus for three whole years. Whilst not all were intellectuals, and it appears most had difficulty understanding some of Jesus teaching, all must have been dramatically affected by the their experience and by the resurrection – and it is believed they were granted special powers at Pentecost. So, why did only John, James and Peter bequeath any informative texts to us – and John's gospel is generally regarded as having been written at least 50 years after the crucifixion? If John was moved to pen his eponymous gospel more than 50 years after following Jesus around Judah, Samaria and Galilee, how come he wrote nothing beforehand? This seems odd, but probably reflects the almost indiscriminate destruction of texts wrought by the Roman Church.

4.16 As we shall see, there is strong evidence of various edits being made to original texts in the New Testament, not necessarily with malevolent intent, as early scribes often felt margin notes marked on a folio were worthy of inclusion in the copy they were writing if they gave a better reflection of, by then, the established dogma.

4.17 But the conclusion of this series will uncover evidence of Jesus teaching that has been largely suppressed for almost two millennia with huge implications for our future existence.

5

The history of history

5.1 The conventional Western understanding of history was highly influenced by the widely acclaimed translation of the Bible into English authorised by King James I. In 1604, James gave the translators instructions intended to guarantee that the new version would conform to the ecclesiology and reflect the episcopal structure of the Church of England and its belief in an ordained clergy. The instruction was to make sure the vernacular version reflected the religious creed of the time – a point not generally appreciated nowadays. Where the scholars found that translation rendered a phrase which contradicted dogma, such phrases were to be modified to align with dogma. Articles of dogma were paramount – if biblical texts disagreed – it was the bible that was wrong! The translation was done by 47 scholars, all of whom were members of the Church of England, and published in 1611.

5.2 Detailed knowledge of the ancient civilizations of Egypt and Mesopotamia had been largely lost by a series of disasters – the fire which destroyed the famous library in Alexandria containing up to 500,000 papyrus scrolls (either by Julius Caesar in 48BC or Aurelian in AD270) and its satellite library, the Serapeum, destroyed on the orders of Pope Theophilus in AD391); the destruction of Babylonian records by the warring successors to Alexander the Great and the loss of academic knowledge in Europe during the thousand years following the collapse of the Western Roman Empire.

5.3 The consequences were profound, "classical" education for a thousand years, from the fall of the Western Roman Empire in AD476 up to Luther's Thesis that launched the Reformation in 1517, was limited to the study of the Roman and Greek civilizations. The ability to translate Egyptian hieroglyphs and cuneiform writing was lost until the 19th Century.

5.4 Accordingly, during the Renaissance centuries, the understanding of ancient history before the Greeks and Romans was based almost entirely on the Bible as the sole historical reference. The publication of the popular King James Version ("KJV") of the bible coincided with the start of the British Empire (the first colonies being founded in India and the Caribbean in the preceding decade), whilst the growth of European empires and the Industrial Revolution brought wealth, global exploration and colonization. Thus, across the English-speaking world, the education of history prior to Imperial Rome, i.e. the period covered by the Old Testament, rested entirely on the KJV translation, with no input from other contemporary sources nor indeed any from far older civilizations.

5.5 Napoleon's troops found the Rosetta Stone in Egypt in 1799 and, with the first transliteration of the hieroglyphs completed in 1822, it became possible to start to understand the mass of original inscriptions left by the Egyptians dating back as far as 3200BC.

5.6 The treasures of Mesopotamia followed soon after. The first translators of cuneiform were George Smith and Henry Rawlinson. Rawlinson's translations of Mesopotamian texts were first presented to the Royal Asiatic Society of London in 1837. In 1846, Smith worked with Layard to excavate Nineveh uncovering the remains of the library of Ashurbanipal (668BC – 627BC), the last king of the Assyrian Empire. A large number of clay tablets were excavated – the British Museum records 30,943 in its collection. From these, Smith was responsible for deciphering The Epic of Gilgamesh and in 1872, famously, the Mesopotamian version of the Flood Story, which until then was thought to be original to the biblical Book of Genesis but copies of the Epic have subsequently been found dating back to 2600BC – around 1,100 years before Moses is generally dated (whom the bible rather implausibly claims was the author of Genesis).

5.7 Huge numbers, possibly totalling a few million, of baked clay tablets have subsequently been recovered from excavations all over the Fertile

Crescent – from many previous centres of early civilisations – including Ur (confirming the origins of Abraham's family given in Genesis), Nineveh (the Royal Library of Ashurbanipal, the last Assyrian king), Babylon, Ugarit (the capital of the Canaanites) and Amarna (the capital built by Akhenaten).

5.8 During the past 150 years or so, researchers and historians have gradually pieced together detailed chronological evidence of the history of the territories referred to in the Old Testament. As individual tablets and descriptions have been recovered and later translated, a steady drip feed of discoveries has continued to rewrite the detailed history, fill in the gaps and provide cross checks and corroboration. Whilst the broad outline of history after the time of Solomon in the biblical record has been broadly corroborated, the biblical texts have been found to contain many anachronisms indicating much later authorship. However, what are generally held to be books dealing with chronological time periods prior to 1000BC have been found to be highly inaccurate – often pointing to far later authorship than conventionally maintained and also to extensive plagiarism – suggestions which many believers find deeply offensive. *But surely, finding and understanding the truth is paramount in dealing with such a profound matter as our origins and our afterlife?*

5.9 The fact that even broad reliability of Old Testament texts can only be established back to around the time of Solomon, is most probably related to the invention of Hebrew writing around 1000BC. Some biblical academics claim evidence of earlier dates but it seems irrefutable that original Hebrew writing adopted the new Phoenician alphabet – and that is well documented as being developed no earlier than 1050BC.

5.10 Armed with knowledge from clay tablets, original writing dating back in some cases up to 5,000 years ago, we can gain clearer understanding of some otherwise puzzling statements – particularly in the Torah, Psalms and Ezekiel. Marrying older source material from ancient clay tablets with the Hebrew texts in the Torah also sheds light on significant facts hidden by translation assumptions used by biblical scholars in the KJV and subsequently.

5.11 To facilitate readers, a summary of the time scales of various ancient civilisations referred to in this booklet is set out below:

PART ONE: GOD, ENKI, RA/MARDUK & YAHWEH

Key events in history of Sumeria, Egypt, Israel and Babylon

Mesopotamia

8000BC – 6000BC	Likely period when shallow waters at head of Persian Gulf were inundated by rising global sea levels, drowning the area most likely to have spawned the legend of the Garden of Eden – see chapter 8.
5300BC – 4100BC	Early proto-Sumerian (non-Semitic people) called Ubaids, drained marshes, developed agriculture, trade, weaving, leatherwork, pottery, masonry and metalwork.
4100BC – 2900BC	Early Sumerian civilisation, centred around Uruk, with earliest written records (clay tablets) dating c 3300BC.
3760BC	Coronation of Etana, 1st king of Sumeria, baseline year 0 of Jewish calendar.
2900BC – 2334BC	Sumerian ascendancy with parallel development of Akkadian (Semitic people) just to north – close symbiotic relationship, many appear to have been bi-lingual.
2334BC – 2083BC	Akkadian kings ascendant, ruling Sumer from 2270BC under King Sargon
2083BC – 1960BC	Third Dynasty of Ur (Sumerians again ruling over Akkadians). During this period, agriculture suffered from rising salinity – reducing crops and the population declined by around 60% as people migrated north up the Tigris and Euphrates rivers. Including Abraham, whose family departed from the capital, Ur, around 1980BC.
2286BC	Founding of Dingir-Ra, Gateway of (the god) Ra, later adopting the Akkadian name Babilim, transliterated as Babylon.
1894BC – 1595BC	First Babylonian (Amorite) Empire – which used Akkadian as written language but kept the Sumerian language and writing for religious & astronomical use.

1821BC – 1793BC	Sin-Muballit, ruler prior to Ra's return.
1792BC – 1750BC	HammuRaBi ruled Babylonian Empire
1594BC – 1155BC	Babylonia ruled by Kassites, an efficient martial tribe exploiting the fall of Babylon to the Hittites. Kassites, believed to originate from Iran, adopted the pre-existing culture, but their power weakened, becoming a vassal state of Egypt - paying tribute to Tuthmose III from c1450BC.
1155BC – 911BC	Re-establishment of Akkadian control after more than a millennium, but weak state repeated attacked by Assyrians and Amoreans.
911BC – 620BC	Babylon part of the Neo-Assyrian Empire until displaced by the Chaldeans.

Egypt

c9600BC	Rise of legacy civilisation with erection of first new megaliths at Giza – see Prequel.
c3600BC	Complex Mummification recipe with dozens of ingredients already standardised 4 centuries before the '1st' pharaoh, with later use unchanged until Ptolemaic period.
3200BC	Menes, founded the First Dynasty in Egypt, preceded by demi-gods
2055BC	Mentuhotep II became Pharaoh and re-established Egyptian rule over Sinai
1971BC – 1926BC	Rule of Senusret I, half-brother of Sarah, Abraham's wife
1720BC – 1550BC	Canaanite rule in eastern Egyptian delta, extending to all Lower Egypt by 1650BC under Hyksos rulers (15th Dynasty)
1750BC – 1400BC	Period in which most place the life of Moses

PART ONE: GOD, ENKI, RA/MARDUK & YAHWEH

1650BC (+/-20)	Best date for meteor destruction of both Jericho and Tell el-Hammam, most likely site for Sodom & Gomorrah, close by (see Part Three). An awesome event which would have created panic and flight to Egypt.
1550BC – 1077BC	New Kingdom period in Egypt – covering 18th, 19th and 20th dynasties, during which Egypt ruled all of what is now Israel, Lebanon and the western half of Syria northwards into the southern edge of Turkey. Egyptian power begun to decline after Ramesses III exhausted Egyptian resources with the defeat of the Sea Peoples in 1177BC, for whom the Egyptians built cities which became the Philistine Pentapolis (broadly where is Gaza today), and by 1077BC with the death of Ramesses XI the Egyptians lost their remaining possessions in Asia.

Israel

c1900BC	Jerusalem, as Urusalem, referred to in Egyptian Execration texts.
c1525BC – c1100BC	Urusalem functioned as an Egyptian military stronghold – see Part Two.
c1050BC	Saul became the first Israelite king according to Bible but other evidence suggests David was the first king.
1003BC	Date that David captured Jerusalem, according to Israeli government sources. Soon followed by adoption of first Hebrew writing based upon Phoenician.
950 BC – 400 BC	*Period during which the Torah was developed, later divided into the 5 books of the Pentateuch.*
911 BC – 620 BC	Assyrian Empire – absorption of Israel, with 10 northern tribes removed in waves between 731BC and 722BC, relocated in different provinces under control of Nineveh (today, Mosul, northern Iraq).
620 BC – 539 BC	Second (Chaldean or Neo-) Babylonian Empire. In 586BC, Nebuchadnezzar, a Chaldean, captured Jerusa-

lem, destroyed the 1st (Solomon's) Temple and took the people of Judah to Babylon – where, the architects and builders were given access to the King's library holding ancient clay tablets of designs of the Amorite temples and palaces which they had to rebuild plus many copies of the epics of Gilgamesh (echoes of Moses); of Ziusudra (the hero of the Flood); and, the 7 tablet creation story, aka the Enuma Elish.

Later control of Babylon

539 BC – 333 BC   Persian Empire. Cyrus the Great captured Babylon in 539BC and allowed the Jews to return to Jerusalem, providing an armed escort – however only a small minority, 4%, are thought to have returned – leaving Babylon as the leading centre of Jewish civilisation for much of the succeeding 1500 years, until c1000AD when the Muslim caliphate enacted harsh anti-Jewish laws causing many to leave.

333 BC   Alexander the Great, captured Babylon, making it part of the Greek Empire

AD 118   Babylon captured by the Romans becoming part of the Roman Empire

5.12   The Mesopotamian civilisations have bequeathed to us the most extensive original records. It is estimated that a few million baked clay tablets, dating back as far as 3300BC, have been recovered from archaeological excavations during the latter part of the 19th and the first half of the 20th centuries. These clay tablets are now housed in museum and university collections, predominantly in the UK, Germany and the US – but only a minority of these have so far been translated. By comparison, the Egyptian records were primarily on papyrus, which fortunately the dry climate has sometimes preserved, or comprised monumental stone inscriptions – often defaced by succeeding dynasties. We have very little original documentation from the Israelites – the largest collection being the Dead Sea Scrolls, 972 whole and partial papyrus and parchment scrolls dating from 408BC up to AD68.

5.13   The only substantive original documents from earlier areas of Israelite habitation comprise cuneiform clay tablets from Ugarit and the 'Amarna Letters'. From Ugarit, located on the Syrian coast north of Lebanon, established around 6000BC and a principal city of Canaan until destroyed around 1200BC, we have a few thousand clay tablets – mainly from four libraries found largely intact – a palace library, a temple library and two private libraries. The 'Amarna letters', comprising clay tablets (unusually for Egyptian government correspondence) written in Akkadian cuneiform, were unearthed in Amarna, Akhenaten's capital, comprising correspondence between the Egyptian central government and regional governors throughout what is now Western Syria, Lebanon, Israel and Sinai – further corroborating Egyptian rule over the entire area referred to in the Exodus during the period when it supposedly took place.

THE HISTORY OF HISTORY

6

Evolution is the primary tool of God

6.1 The outright hatred many Christians, ironically including many Americans, profess for evolution is particularly puzzling.

6.2 There is plenty of evidence that God designed the evolution of stellar systems to forge planets as captive satellites. In turn, it seems planets come endowed with usually multiple captive moons both to keep gravitational forces 'stirring' planetary cores (as molten cores help maintain magnetospheres which then retain planetary atmospheres) and to help regulate climates. Inter-stellar dust, slowly drawn together into clumps by gravity, would naturally start to rotate as matter coalesced to form an increasingly dense core surrounded by a similarly rotating field of other materials spinning in a plane around it. Gravity would eventually cause the star to ignite as the increasing density of the core led to rising pressure and rising heat. The combustion of hydrogen in fusion reactions, to form helium whilst emitting light and heat, thereby producing energy and light essential to the development of intelligent life.

6.3 Humankind was blessed by having its star form on the edge of a large galaxy, remote from the broiling radiation of x-rays and gamma rays at the intensively active core of a galaxy and in the relatively less dense outer areas with far less frequent supernovae. This is critical, as a supernova would sterilise any life form within a distance of 20m light years – and we have evidence from ocean deposits that life on Earth has suffered from exactly such impacts in the past. The strongest recent radiation bombardment occurred only 2.59 million years ago – when humanoids already roamed on Earth. This event witnessed the extinction of many species and is recognised as marking the end of the Pliocene Epoch. If one showed the history of planet Earth as a 24 hour clock, this extinction level radiation event would occur at 23:59:12 – frighteningly recent!

6.4   The early atmosphere of planets would likely comprise hydrogen, nitrogen and sulphides. But the beginnings of organic life would yield oxygen and the development of lichen, vegetation and trees – steadily increasing the proportion of free oxygen as well as carbon dioxide.

6.5   The prior evolution of a supportive eco-system is a pre-requisite for the existence of a complex intelligent life form – unless it is highly dependent upon technology. Human kind had the good fortune, or providence, to emerge into a veritable Garden of Eden. Fruit, vegetables, cereals, fish and animals had evolved in great abundance and diversity – each in turn requiring overlapping eco-systems to evolve and prosper.

6.6   The domestication of almost all food crops and farmed animals appears to have originated in Mesopotamia and spread out therefrom. The impact on civilisation of the abundance of such domesticated foodstuffs in the Eurasian landmass compared with the sub Saharan Africa, the Americas and Australia, which all had very few species, is described by Jared Diamond (a Pulitzer Prize winner) in his excellent work "Guns, Germs and Steel". Diamond's analysis identifies that whilst humanity was fortunate to evolve into an ecosystem supporting a vast array of flora and fauna, the transition to large scale civilization required very specific features. Humans had to transition from hunter-gatherers to settled farming communities in order to generate surpluses which freed people to specialize in activities apart from maintaining sustenance and to support population growth. But this transition is predicated by key conditions, including: (i) plants that contain high levels of protein that endures storage; (ii) climatic conditions that permit storage without unacceptable spoilage; and, (iii) available breeds of animal docile enough to domesticate and versatile enough to survive captivity whilst yielding quality meat and other products – dairy products, hides, etc. Stark differences in the availability of suitable plants and animals account for the different early evolution of humans in the Americas compared with Eurasia. Eurasia enjoyed barley, wheat and several rich pulses, plus goats, sheep and cattle. Eurasian grains were richer in protein, easier to sow and easier to store than American maize or bananas. South America, with potatoes and docile llama, might have fared better but never smelted ores harder than gold and silver and never invented the wheel.

6.7   Thus even with the huge advantages of the positioning of our sun, our planet relative to our sun and 4.54 billion years to evolve a complex eco-system to support intelligent life – the absence or abundance of crops and animal species suitable to support the switch from hunter-gatherer to farmer and thence to specialised communities and ultimately industrialisation depended on the abundance of plants and animals suited to domestication.

6.8   If one believes that God created the universe, it is logical to also believe he created it for a purpose. Certainly, the intellectual fun of defining all the physical laws to generate the unlimited variety of galaxies, solar systems and planets with an infinite variety of geology and landscapes – must have provided God with enthralling entertainment over the past 13 billion years!! But apart from that, I think we would like to assume that God also wanted to evolve intelligent life forms that he could have a relationship with.

6.9   Are we the only, or perhaps the first, intelligent life form that God has evolved? Such an assumption seems staggeringly arrogant – in a universe where, as Carl Sagan famously put it, 'there are more stars than the grains of sand on any beach you can imagine'. The very clear probability is that God has watched other intelligent life forms evolve on numerous planets – indeed some will be more advanced and probably less evil than humans. This issue has even been addressed by the Vatican in recent years. On 23 July 2014, Rosana Ubanell from Voxxi News reported that due to advances in scientific detection methods for the discovery of extraterrestrial life, Pope Francis wants to be ready with a statement about "First Contact". Ubanell reported that Pope Francis is preparing a statement about extraterrestrial life and its theological implications. Details have yet to be officially announced but the Vatican's interest in extraterrestrial life is well documented through recent astrobiology conferences the Vatican Observatory has sponsored or participated in. Father Guy Consolmagno, a Jesuit astronomer, was awarded the Carl Sagan Science Medal in 2014 by the American Astronomical Society. Pope Francis, a fellow Jesuit, regularly consults with Consolmagno and other leading Vatican astronomers about scientific issues. It is likely that Pope Francis is preparing an "Urbi et Orbi" speech – Latin for "to the city [of Rome] and the world" – about First Contact with extraterrestrial life.

6.10 The Vatican's scientific interest in extraterrestrial life was publicly revealed for the first time in May 2008 when the head of the Vatican Observatory, Fr Gabriel Funes, also a Jesuit and also an Argentine, gave an interview to the Vatican newspaper, L'Osservatore Romano. Funes made a series of startling statements about how extraterrestrial life is likely to be more ethically evolved than humans, and can be welcomed as brothers. In his interview, which was titled "The extraterrestrial is my brother," Funes said that intelligent extraterrestrial life may not have experienced a 'fall', and may be "free from Original Sin... [remaining] in full friendship with their creator."

6.11 Not only might other intelligent life forms be more ethically evolved but potentially their civilizations might have evolved over an unimaginable period of time. In January 2015, a group of astronomers led by Tiago Campante of Birmingham University, UK, announced the discovery of five rocky planets around Kepler 444, a star some 117 light years from Earth. The most striking discovery was the age of the star, calculated at 11.2 billion years using asteroseismology. This is the most ancient planetary system yet found, indicating planets started forming quite early in the life of the universe. Whilst terraforming and eco-systems capable of sustaining intelligent life took 3 to 4 billion years to evolve on Earth – theoretically, making a similar allowance would still allow intelligent life elsewhere to have flowered for 7 or 8 billion years versus our 10,000 years or so.

6.12 As with the physical characteristics of our universe, given the truly staggering characteristics, it seems to me highly likely that God had a role in designing an operating system to support life. As we considered in chapter 3, Earthly DNA might be just one example of these operating systems. Having set the rules, God appears to have relied upon natural evolution to evolve the majestic variety of life forms on each planet with suitable conditions to support life.

EVOLUTION IS THE PRIMARY TOOL OF GOD

7

The creation of the Torah (first 5 books of the OT)

7.1 The Torah was originally a single scroll, it was only divided into five books around 200BC.

7.2 Many Christians and many Jews believe that Moses wrote the Torah. However, it is very clear that no part of the Torah could have been written by Moses as the Hebrew alphabet was not invented until around 1000BC. Hebrew script is clearly based upon the very first phonetic alphabet, Phoenician – which can be traced back to around 1050BC. If Moses even existed, and there is much to indicate he is a fictional hero, he would have written in Egyptian hieroglyphics. If so, given the sacred nature of the text, it is very unlikely that the early Israelite priests would have translated the text into archaic Hebrew. This can be compared with religious texts we have from the first Babylonian Empire, from 1894BC to 1595BC, all of whose sacred texts were written in Sumerian, from whence the beliefs had originated, with texts specifying that they were true copies of earlier texts going back more than a 1000 years earlier. Furthermore, if the Torah had been translated into archaic Hebrew, as a few parts are clearly written in – then why would large parts have been further rewritten into Classical Hebrew – whilst leaving some sections in archaic Hebrew?

7.3 Language, style and grammar alone strongly suggest most of the Torah was written around a thousand years after Moses is believed to have lived. From the content, there is a lot of evidence that the Torah was mainly written during the exile in Babylon, between 590BC and 530BC, with many historians suggesting that some parts were heavily influenced by Greek writings which became widely known in Israel after conquest by Alexander the Great in 330BC – around a 100 years before the Torah was split into five scrolls.

7.4 As well as using Hebrew from different periods, the style of writing differs markedly, suggesting a number of different writers whilst evidence of redaction (subsequent editing) occurs in many places, combining Classical Hebrew (used during the Exile and up to the Greek conquest, a period from 590BC to 332BC) with more archaic Hebrew, in parts dating back as far as around 950BC (reign of Solomon).

7.5 Academics have studied the Torah for centuries to try to understand it. Dating back to 1651, Thomas Hobbes cited various passages that implied Moses could not be the author. In the 18th Century many other writers also concluded the same, including Baruch Spinoza, Richard Simon and John Hampden. From 1780 Johann Eichhorn started analysing the entire Pentateuch, concluding by 1822 that Moses had not written any of it. Many others worked on the issue, concluding similar writing styles in Joshua, Judges, Kings and Samuel. By 1853, Hermann Hufield had concluded that there were at least four major contributors, a number of lesser contributors plus a final editor or redactor.

7.6 Scholars, of which Wellhausen is regarded as the original exponent, attempted to identify the sequence and dates of the four major contributors – his identification, which has largely stood the test of time, comprises:

- the Yahwist source (J) written around 950BC in Judah;

- the Elohist source (E) written around 850BC in Israel;

- the Deuteronomist (D) written around 620BC in Jerusalem during reign of Josiah;

- the Priestly source (P) written around 550BC by Kohanim, Jewish priests in Babylon.

Whilst the precise details have been widely challenged, the terminology and insights continue to provide the framework for modern theories on the origin of the Torah and the Old Testament texts in general.

THE CREATION OF THE TORAH (FIRST 5 BOOKS OF THE OT)

7.7 An evolutionary pattern emerges, early Israelite religion was natural and free from law as expressed by the Yahwist and Elohist sources. Its cycles were related to the agricultural year and its priesthood was universal and worship could take place anywhere. Later the Deuteronomist cut off the sacred festivals from nature and gave new dates based on mathematical calculations. The Priestly source fixed the festivals on precise dates in the calendar, demanded centralised worship (under their control) and the priesthood became the exclusive right of the Levites.

7.8 The Yahwist source is defined as narrative in style, making up half of Genesis and half of Exodus plus fragments of Numbers, with a special focus on the territory of Judah. This source presents a history of theology rather than a timeless philosophical theology. The Yahwist is focused on the Israelites as Yahweh's own people, a provider and a protector, making many personal appearances with many cycles of sin, punishment and mercy.

7.9 The Elohist source uses more generic titles such as Elohim rather than the personal Yahweh, who is more impersonal appearing through dreams, prophets and angels. The Elohist often repeats narratives and accounts for a third of Genesis, half of Exodus plus fragments of Numbers.

7.10 The Deuteronomist source, believed to have written Deuteronomy and parts of Joshua, Judges and Kings, takes the form of a number of lectures about the Mosaic Law as well as recapitulating the narrative of Exodus and Numbers. The destruction of Israel and Judah being portrayed as retaliation for disobedience – the intent of the Deuteronomist being to show the exiles that they were in the second stage of a cycle of apostasy, punishment, repentance and delivery – and that the pattern required the exiles simply to turn back to Yahweh.

7.11 The Priestly source, is believed to have written about 20% of Genesis (including chapter 1), substantial sections of Exodus and Numbers and almost all of Leviticus and is dated during the Exile or up to 100 years after the return from Exile. The Priestly source includes many lists, genealogies, dates, numbers and laws – and duplicates a lot of narrative written by earlier contributors whilst altering the details to stress the importance of the priesthood. Yahweh is often viewed as distant and unmerciful – but very interested in ritual. This source shifts mediation with Yahweh from kingship to the priesthood, and at a central place of worship. The Priestly source seems to abruptly demote Moses, just before Leviticus, in the closing verses of Exodus, 40.35 states that Moses, who had led the Israelites out of "bondage" and been the sole person with whom Yahweh was prepared to meet and speak to, burning bush, Mount Sinai, etc., having just laboured to build the Tabernacle – was now abruptly prohibited from entering it to meet Yahweh. In exhaustive detail, Leviticus sets out how Israelites should conduct themselves, be subject to inspection by the priests and the extensive offerings of food to be provided for offering sacrifices to Yahweh, who seems to have a strong desire for the aroma of roast meats, and which are to be consumed by the priests when Yahweh is absent. Close similarities between the rituals and sacrifices made to Marduk by the priests in Babylon and those described for Yahweh suggest one was strongly influenced by the other – did the Babylonian theologians decide to copy the rituals of those exiled from Judah? Perhaps the influence flowed in the other direction?

7.12   It is interesting that after setting out extensive requirements for sacrifices of choice foods, Numbers 15.5 records that once in the Promised Land, every sacrifice of a lamb should be accompanied by a "quarter of a hin of wine". Authorities differ over the definition of a "hin" – Collins says 3.5 litres; Websters says 5.7 litres and the International Standard Bible says around 8 litres. Therefore a quarter hin may amount to 1 to 2 litres – to accompany every sacrifice of a lamb, as a wave offering – which is then left for the priests to quaff !! No wonder, the following chapter of Numbers reports a rebellion by other branches of the Levite tribe and some of the Reuben tribe who also want to be eligible for the priesthood.

7.13   Different authors in different areas writing at different periods would explain the numerous repeated narratives with slightly differing details, reflecting old oral traditions having evolved over time, as in:

- Two creation stories in Genesis.

- Two descriptions of the Abrahamic covenant.

- Two stories of the naming of Isaac.

- Two instances where Abraham introduced his wife Sarah as his sister.

- Two stories of Jacob traveling to Mesopotamia

THE CREATION OF THE TORAH (FIRST 5 BOOKS OF THE OT)

- Two stories of a revelation at Beth-el to Jacob.

- Two accounts of God changing Jacob's name to Israel

- Two instances where Moses extracted water from two different rocks at two different locations called Meribah.

My own theory to explain these duplications is that for the creation story, and Adam to Noah, one version came from Israelite oral traditions originating from Abraham and the other from discovery of the original written texts in Babylon during the Exile. From Abraham onwards, different tribes may have developed variant oral traditions. Uncertain which was the more accurate led the priests to include both versions.

7.14 The Rabbinical style of writing uses 40 years as a standard generational period – so many periods are described as 40 years – the reigns of David and Solomon, the three periods of Moses life and God's prophesy of the length of the period to be spent in foreign lands at 400 years – is a multiple. This reduces the historical accuracy and surely disqualifies labelling these texts as being "inerrant".

7.15 Debate will continue to rage over by whom and when the Torah and its immediately succeeding books were written. However, various statements in the Torah provide proof of its late authorship and the widespread adoption of older pagan practices and beliefs in its drafting.

Late authorship

7.16 The writers of the Torah were very unsure about who ruled Egypt during the period covered by Moses – so it seems that they tried to avoid mistakes by never mentioning the names of any Pharaohs or many places in Egypt.

7.17 However, where places and peoples are mentioned – they reveal poor knowledge of local history. A few illustrative examples indicate just how poorly informed, something which severely undermines claims of biblical inerrancy:

(i) At the time of the Babylonian Exile, Israelites would have known Babylon ruled all of the Fertile Crescent down to roughly the current border of Egypt in northern Sinai, they may also have remem-

PART ONE: GOD, ENKI, RA/MARDUK & YAHWEH

bered that Israel and Judah once formed a single kingdom under David and Solomon. However, the writers of the Torah, Joshua and Judges seem to have been unaware that almost throughout the second millennium BC, the middle of which period they seem to have placed Moses and the conquest of the Promised Land, the entire area in which all the action takes place was a settled part of the Egyptian Empire – and for long periods the Egyptian border with Babylonia was the River Orontes, running through the Bekaa valley in Lebanon.

(ii) One example of many references that rule out authorship by Moses, whilst strongly indicating drafting during the Babylonian exile is the reference to Abraham being from "Ur of the Chaldeans" (Genesis 11:28). The Chaldeans first appear as a tribe migrating into the area around Ur between 940BC and 860BC – more than 1,000 years after Abraham left! They were subjugated by the Assyrians, with the very first historical reference to the Chaldeans occurring in 852 BC, in the records of the Assyrian king Shalmaneser III who mentions the Chaldeans invading the south eastern extremes of Babylonia. The Chaldeans were later involved in the downfall of Nineveh with the first Neo-Babylonian kings being Chaldeans. The fact that Nebuchadnezzar was a Chaldean again underlines the authorship as being during the Babylonian exile.

(iii) References to negotiations with the king of the Edomites (Numbers 20.14) sound odd as the kingdom of Edom only existed briefly in the 7th century BC before being destroyed by the Babylonians.

(iv) Likewise, in Genesis 21:32 and 21:34, Abraham speaks of the Philistines, and again in Exodus 13.18, are references to the Israelites of the Exodus seeking to avoid the Philistines – who only arrived centuries later. In 1178BC ferocious warriors from the Greek islands armed with deadly new iron weapons destroyed most of the old Bronze Age civilisations. Known as the Sea Peoples, they rampaged through Turkey destroying the Hittites and swung south through Syria, Lebanon and Canaan until defeated by the Egyptians under Ramesses II in 1177BC. Ramesses then absorbed these warrior tribes into his empire, building the five walled cities of the Pentapolis (today's Gaza Strip) for them to live.

THE CREATION OF THE TORAH (FIRST 5 BOOKS OF THE OT)

(v) In Numbers 33:35 and Deuteronomy 2:8 references are made to camping at Ezion-Geber, however excavation of this town has found it was only established around 800BC and occupied until around 400BC – and so was a place existing at the time of the Exile in Babylon but only many centuries after Moses supposed existence.

(vi) Donald Redford writes in 'Egypt, Canaan and Israel in Ancient Times', p257: "There is no mention of an Egyptian empire encompassing the eastern Mediterranean, no marching Egyptian armies bent on punitive campaigns, no countermarching Hittite forces, no resident Egyptian governors, no Egyptianised kinglets ruling Canaanite cities, no burdensome tribute or cultural exchange. Of the latest and most disastrous migration of the second millennium, that of the Sea Peoples, the Torah and Joshua are silent; Genesis and Exodus find the Philistines already settled in the land at the time of Abraham." (The best date for Abraham's family departing Ur is 1980BC, however, the Philistines only arrived in what is now Gaza, in 1177BC.)

(vii) Discussing the period of the biblical judges, supposedly from around 1450BC to 1050BC, Redford also observes that whilst the Egyptians were dominant over the Levant (covering Sinai, Israel, Lebanon, Jordan and western Syria) throughout this period, "our Egyptian sources mention neither the patriarchs, Joshua, nor his successors – while the Bible says absolutely nothing about the Egyptian empire ruling everywhere the Israelites were supposedly occupying. The biblical writers had no idea how to depict the appropriate history of Egyptians in Canaan, nor had the Egyptians ever heard of the patriarchs and judges who supposedly engaged in such dramatic behaviours as recorded in the Old Testament.

(viii) Around the period when most biblical scholars (believing an Exodus occurred) place the event, the Egyptian Empire was arguably at its height in terms of geographical coverage. Thutmose III, who reigned from 1479BC until 1425BC led a number of successful campaigns against the Mitanni and the Hurrians in what today is Northern Syria and south eastern Turkey. The extensive records of his campaigns refer to him making combined land and naval attacks and sailing his forces up the Euphrates. This would mean that throughout the Exodus and the occupation of the Promised Land, the Israelites never left Egyptian territory!

7.18   Fundamentally, these errors and anachronisms show the Old Testament is far from historically accurate. Which, adopting the logic of the inerrantists, suggests that if the 'easy to prove' details are so wrong – what faith can one place in the theological claims which are unverifiable.

Adoption of older pagan practices and beliefs

7.19   Important elements of the story in the Torah can be traced to older belief systems.

7.20   Some historians believe that the Ten Commandments originated from ancient Egyptian religion, and postulate that the Biblical Jews borrowed the concept during their Exodus from Egypt. Chapter 125 of the Book of the Dead (the Papyrus of Ani) includes a list of things to which a man must swear in order to enter the afterlife. These sworn statements bear a remarkable resemblance to the Ten Commandments in their nature and their phrasing. These statements include "not have I defiled the wife of man," "not have I committed murder," "not have I committed theft," "not have I lied," "not have I cursed god," "not have I borne false witness," and "not have I abandoned my parents." The Book of the Dead has additional requirements relating to Egyptian gods, but, of course, it doesn't require worship of Yahweh.

7.21   We can trace the origin of the 7 day week back to the Sumerians during the third millennium BC. The idea of the Sabbath, as a day of rest and worship once a week, looks a direct take on the Babylonian "shabattu" for the weekly day of rest. Tablets have been unearthed from Babylon recording a calendar of feasts and sacrifices specifying the 7th, 14th, 21st and 28th days of every month be set apart as days on which no work should be done, on which the king would not change his robes, nor mount his chariot, nor render legal decisions nor eat of boiled or roasted meats. The pattern is lunisolar with 12 months of alternating periods of 29 and 30 days plus a few odd days at the end of the year. However, whilst the practise of a sabbath dates from Sumerian times, the Sumerians only used "shabattu" for the monthly worship on the day of the full Moon of their chief local deity, the Moon god (in Akkadian called "Sin") whose realm included Sinai. Other tablets dating from King Shulgi who ruled from Ur and is famous for completing the Ziggurat of Ur, describe the Sumerian monthly "shabattu". As Shugli reigned from 2029BC to 1982BC, he appears to have been Abraham's king until his family migrated north. The importance of the monthly Shabattu, as recorded in Exodus, is commented on in section 12. The adoption in the Torah of a weekly Sabbath rather than a lunar monthly Sabbath again points to authorship being primarily in Babylon during the Exile, as a real Moses would only have known of the monthly ritual.

7.22 The Romans always used an 8 day week until Christians started using a 7 day week and it was not until AD321 that Emperor Constantine officially adopted a 7 day week throughout the Roman Empire.

7.23 Many aspects of Dionysus worship and myth seem to have been incorporated in the story of Moses – see section 11 for more details. The myths of Dionysus contributed many attributes concerning wine.

7.24 The close resemblance between the celebration of the Feast of the Booths (Tabernacles) and the Feast of Thyrsophoria in honour of Bacchus/Dionysus was noted by Plutarch (AD45 to AD120) who described the common features – booths of palm branches and ivy; with Levites playing cithens; the mitre, tunic and bells on the vestments of the high priests and the timing in late September – to coincide with the first vintage. Deuteronomy 16.13 specifies the Feast of Booths to be held "when ingathering from threshing and your winepress is completed".

7.25 There are also many attributes of solar worship. Many have drawn attention to Psalm 104, which seems to combine Akhenaten's "Hymn to the Sun" in verses 1 to 18, with worship of the Canaanite storm god in verses 20 to 30. (Paul Dion, "Yahweh as Storm god and Sun god"). References to Moses face shining (after meeting Yahweh) use the Hebrew word 'qaran' which means 'to shine', 'to send out rays' and 'to display or grow horns' – hence old Christian depictions of Moses with horns (e.g. by Michelangelo c1514). The horns have multiple meanings – serving to indicate Moses was "son of the cow" (Moses great grandmother was Leah, meaning 'cow') and the link to the Golden Calf. Dionysus is also sometimes depicted with horns.

7.26 Surprisingly, a number of ancient synagogues have been found with images of a Sun god, surrounded by the 12 signs of the zodiac – at Hammath Tiberias, Sepphoris, Beth Alpha, Naaran, Susiya, Ussefiyeh and Ein Gedi. Philo (a Jewish historian based in Alexandria 1st century

BC) and Josephus (a Jewish historian, contemporary of Jesus and author of the only surviving contemporary account of Jesus outside the Gospels) both wrote that the 12 tribes of Israel were based upon the zodiac. The historical evidence indicates that the Israelites at the time of the Kings had emerged from Amorites (West Semitic people from Babylonia), Hittites, (your Mother was a Hittite and your Father was an Amorite – per Ezekiel 16), Canaanites, Hapiru (from whence the term 'Hebrew' was derived) and the Shasu of Yhw. The concept of the 12 tribes undertaking an exodus from Egypt is mythical and conveniently the authors of the Torah (working in Babylon) despatched most of the excess tribes a century before doing most of the writing, care of the Assyrians who supposedly marched them all to Nineveh, where they were conveniently written out of history.

7.27 An interesting angle on the writers of the Torah has been developed by Harold Bloom, an American Jew who learned Yiddish and Hebrew before he learnt English. In his publication 'The Western Canon', Bloom analyses the writing of the supposed four principal authors of the Torah, conventionally identified as J, E, P and D. Like others, he agrees with Wellhausen's assessment (see 7.6) that J was the oldest but, more controversially, that J was a woman who had originally written a literary work rather than a religious text. Bloom suggested that J could have been a daughter or granddaughter in the court of King David's successors, Solomon or Rehoboam – which also agrees with Wellhausen's dating of around 950BC. One reviewer of his work suggested J was Bathsheba – one of David's wives and Solomon's mother. Bloom identifies Ezra as the scribe who combined the scrolls of the Torah into a single work around 444BC. Only a few centuries later did the Torah come to its present five book format.

Conclusions

7.28 The evolution of the Torah must have come from numerous narratives of early Hebrew tribes and their leaders, probably in the form of songs and poems, initially transmitted orally. Gradually some tales were gathered into cycles dealing with various common periods or individuals and which were used as the elements of history weaved into detailed sections of religious ritual written in Babylon to create the national foundation myth to finally establish monotheism and consolidate the priesthood in its natural controlling position in ancient society.

THE CREATION OF THE TORAH (FIRST 5 BOOKS OF THE OT)

7.29　When the exiled priests in Babylon found parallel texts describing their creation story and the story of the Flood in the Enuma Elish with unerringly similar details to their pre-existing sections of the Torah written from Solomon's reign onwards, they simply added parts into the Torah roll creating the sections which appear as duplications of the same themes. What the exiled priests found were accurate copies of the identical texts that were revered by Abraham's family before they departed from Ur 1,500 years previously. Variations between the two versions of creation and of the Flood reveal the extent to which oral tradition was able to maintain accurate details over at least 1000 years (Abraham to Solomon) before being committed to writing.

8

What is the Genesis story of creation?

8.1　The story of creation in Genesis (Genesis 1-3) is often quoted by atheists and less dogmatic Christians as evidence of the bible's fallibility. Surprisingly, we now have detailed knowledge of where and when this story of creation was introduced into the Torah. Fundamentally, it is not an explanation of the creation of the universe but is much more narrowly focused on describing the evolution of certain bodies in our solar system – namely Earth, Tiamat (the planet whose remnants now form the asteroid belt), Earth's moon and an intruder planet with a very eccentric orbit, named as Nibiru which was understood to spend most of its orbit far beyond Pluto. Recently, astronomers have concluded that at least one significant sized body, with a mass a few times greater than Earth, does indeed orbit far beyond Pluto – deduced from the evidence of its gravitational perturbation of other outer planets. Genesis also nods at terraforming on Earth and goes on to populate the Earth with instantly created and fully evolved lifeforms.

8.2　A sharp eyed reader may challenge my giving the name 'Tiamat' to the planet now generally believed to have orbited our Sun between Mars and Jupiter. This name comes from our understanding of the Sumerian records – the big question is how they knew about the asteroid belt – the largest member of which, Ceres, was officially only discovered in 1801. And, further, how did they know the belt was formed from the debris of a planet? The advanced cosmological knowledge of the Sumerians raises many questions.

8.3 Chapter 2 and 3 of Genesis, describing the Garden of Eden and telling of man's period in it, point to distant folk memories of ancient events affecting human society which long pre-date recorded history. Recently, we have identified evidence which lends support to some of the detail in the biblical story of the Garden of Eden.

8.4 This chapter will touch on specific details of the three main themes embedded in Genesis chapters 1 to 3 – the formation of planet Earth, the creation of Man and the Garden of Eden

8.5 One phrase, referring to 'the waters above the firmament and the waters below the firmament' has long puzzled readers and particularly translators – sometimes leading to the conclusion that it referred to the emergence of continents. Genesis 1:6-8 states *"And God said, Let there be a firmament in the midst of the waters, and let it divide the waters from the waters. And God made the firmament, and divided the waters which were under the firmament from the waters which were above the firmament: and it was so. And God called the firmament Heaven."* Today, our knowledge of our solar system and the identification of translation errors reveals the true meaning. It is now understood that "firmament" was a translation from Hebrew by 15th Century translators puzzled by the Hebrew terms *"rakia"* which literally meant 'hammered out bracelet' and *"shamaim"* referred to 'the watery place'.

8.6 In Hebrew, Genesis 1:8 explicitly states that it is this "hammered out bracelet" that the Lord had named "heaven" *(shamaim)*. The Akkadian texts also called this celestial zone "the hammered bracelet" *(rakkis)*, resulting from a celestial collision that destroyed the planet previously orbiting between Mars and Jupiter. The collision resulted in one very large chunk which spun into an orbit closer to the sun – becoming our planet Earth, and a trail of wreckage littering the orbit of the former planet – what we now call the asteroid belt. The Sumerian sources are clear that "the hammered bracelet" refers to the asteroid belt rather than the general concept of 'the heavens'.

8.7 Thus the asteroid belt and planet Earth are the "Heaven and Earth" of both the original Sumerian texts and the long subsequent (up to 3,000 years later) biblical texts.

8.8 Having understood 'firmament' means the asteroid belt, academics then puzzled by what 'waters' existed above and below the 'firmament'? Even 20 years ago, most scientists did not think water existed in any quantity on any other planets in our solar system – the inner planets were too hot or arid and the gas giants too turbulent. Now we know differently. In the Prequel to this series we looked at the history of Mars with its ancient weather and large oceans; water has been detected on Venus; large volumes of water ice have been detected in the asteroid belt, in the rings of Jupiter and Neptune, some of the moons of Neptune and on Pluto.

8.9 On 11th August 2020, The Guardian reported on the first analysis of data collected by the Nasa spacecraft Dawn – obtained from only 35km above the surface of Ceres. Ceres, with a diameter of 940km, is now designated as a 'dwarf planet', same as Pluto, and constitutes the largest remnant of Taimat remaining in the asteroid belt. Previously believed to be a barren space rock, Ceres is now found to be an ocean world with reservoirs of sea water beneath its surface. Infrared imaging has revealed the presence of hydrohalite – a material common in sea ice but has never before been found except on Earth. Maria Cristina De Sanctis, from Rome's Istituto Nazionale di Astrofisica said hydrohalite was a clear sign Ceres used to have sea water. This further supports the theory that Earth and Ceres share a common parent body – Tiamat.

8.10 Clearly the widespread occurrence of water will be a boon to space travel – but again it would be interesting to learn how the Sumerians gained this knowledge? In Genesis Revisited, Zecharia Sitchin has written a comprehensive summary of the original Sumerian explanation of the history of the formation of Earth within our solar system, drawing out the parallels with Genesis.

8.11 The true origin of the Genesis tale of creation was first indicated by the recovery of texts found in 1849 in the library of the Assyrian king, Ashurbanipal, in Nineveh (near Kirkuk, in Kurdish Iraq); which reads, in some parts word for word, the tale of Genesis. The Sumerian creation story is generally referred to as the 'Enuma Elish', after the first phrase of the text – which translates as 'When in the Heights'.

8.12 Older versions of the Enuma Elish, from the First Babylonian Empire, were found and in 1876 George Smith of the British Museum published a translation entitled The Chaldean Genesis. The title is confusing as it suggests the text was Chaldean (i.e. from the Second 'Chaldean' Babylonian Empire – rather than from the First – some 1200 years earlier). The founders of the first Babylonian empire were Amorite tribes, the found-

PART ONE: GOD, ENKI, RA/MARDUK & YAHWEH

ers of the second were the Chaldeans, who emerged from lands west of Ur. (Hence the revealing biblical reference that Abraham came from 'Ur of the Chaldeans' – another proof that Genesis dates from the time of the Exile.)

8.13 As described in chapter 14, Egyptian records tell of their most important god, Ra, disappearing around 1990BC after which he became known as Amen (the hidden one) and pharaohs started adopting 'Amen' as part of their name. Many centuries earlier, a city dedicated to Ra had been established in Sumeria named Dingur Ra (the Gateway of Ra). Looking at Babylonian king lists, it appears that Ra re-established his base in Dingur Ra around 1750BC. This is shown by the abrupt change in throne names from father to son. After Ra took up residence in Babylon, **Sin**-Muballit was succeeded by his son taking the name Hammu*ra*bi. Ra changed the name of the city to Babylon and adopted the name Marduk, hence we find his priests changed the name of the supreme god to Marduk in new Babylonian versions of the Enuma Elish. Note: at the time, this divine succession was also seen as the zodiacal precession from Taurus to Ares – as Sin, the son of Enlil, the Bull of Heaven, ceded power to Ra, whose sign was the Ram. This use of the symbol of the ram may be an early example of clever branding – Ra knew the age would witness the emergence of the constellation of Ares to mark the dawn.

8.14 The technique of editing the 'globally recognized' creation story to glorify your national god was next adopted by the Assyrians. The excavations of Nineveh between 1902 and 1914, uncovered tablets with the Assyrian version of the creation epic, in which the name of Ashur, the Assyrian national god, was substituted for that of the Babylonian Marduk.

8.15 As partial copies begun to be found from the ruins of several much older Sumerian cities, it begun to be understood that the Sumerian tale of creation was the sacred foundation myth of Mesopotamia dating back as far as the 4th millennia BC. It was L. W. King who, in 1902, in his work The Seven Tablets of Creation, showed that the various fragments add up to seven tablets; six of them relate the creation process; the seventh tablet is entirely devoted to the exaltation of "the Lord Most High". The prior existence of the seven tablet structure points to the origin of the seven-day timetable for creation found in Genesis.

8.16 Our understanding of the Enuma Elish was initially confused by mis-

WHAT IS THE GENESIS STORY OF CREATION?

understanding its genealogy. The first translation, by George Smith in 1876, was from an almost complete set of its seven tablets recovered from the library of Ashurbanipal in Nineveh – indicating it might date from around the 8th century BC. This quickly led to the assumption that the Enuma Elish had been modelled on the creation tale in Genesis which at that time was widely believed to have been written by Moses many centuries earlier.

8.17 The progressive discovery of older and older versions of the Enuma Elish have revealed its evolution over many millennia prior to Ashurbanipal. These historical facts have still not filtered through to many Christian apologists – who still routinely state that, when the Enuma Elish was written, the author drew heavily upon a pre-existing Book of Genesis, quoting the discovery in Nineveh.

8.18 Fascinating records recovered from Babylon explain how the Enuma Elish clearly formed the basis for the drafting of Genesis by the Kohanim, Jewish priests in Babylon during the Exile. Records that indicate that Nebuchadnezzar specifically rounded up Jewish architects, builders and stonemasons from Jerusalem because he wanted to rebuild the palaces and temples from the first Babylonian Empire that were, at that time, over 1000 years old and in serious disrepair. The King's library apparently held tablets showing the original building specifications and the Jewish craftsmen were given free access to Nebuchadnezzar's library to study and work from these drawings – where most likely they also read the Enuma Elish.

8.19 The Exiles from Judah would also have witnessed the annual New Year festival where the Babylonian priests read aloud the entire Enuma Elish. It was the most hallowed religious-political-scientific document of the time; it was read out annually as a central part of the New Year rituals, and players re-enacted the tale in passion plays to bring its import home to the masses. The clay tablets on which they were written were prized possessions of temples and royal libraries in antiquity.

8.20 The first five books of the Old Testament, the Torah, state that the author was Moses, whose very existence is disputed but most would date to around 1500BC. However, Hebrew writing did not emerge until around 1000BC and the language of the most of the Torah is not early archaic Hebrew but classical Hebrew – the language of the Exile to Babylon

596BC to 538BC.

8.21 As Sitchin concludes, one day the Creationists may come to realize that what the editors and compilers of the Book of Genesis did was no different from what the Babylonians and the Assyrians had done – see 8.12 and 8.13 above. The Levites used the most respected scientific source of their time, the Epic of Creation, shortened and edited it, and made it the foundation of a national religion glorifying Yahweh "who is in the Heavens and on Earth." Ironically, it had travelled full circle, as the same Epic of Creation was almost certainly also revered by Abraham's family in Ur. And, indeed, as we shall see, my conclusions indicate that the Yahweh worshipped by the Israelites was initially a son (and later a grandson) of the same Lord Most High that was worshipped by Abraham and his parents – with evidence enabling us to identify which individuals became associated with incarnations of the Hebrew god in successive generations.

8.22 As our knowledge of the composition and history of our solar system improves, we are surprised to find hints that such knowledge was already known to an ancient civilization up to 6,000 years ago. Most people regard the Sumerian Enuma Elish as a myth about ancient pagan gods. As we found in the Prequel, 'gods' is a misleading description – a core of elite humans may be a more accurate description. We continue to find surprising evidence that the Sumerian creation myth contains some factual knowledge. Whilst some scientists and theologians are now aware of the Mesopotamian origin of Genesis, they remain stubborn in denying there is any scientific value in these ancient texts. It cannot be science, they hold, because "it should be obvious by the nature of things that none of these stories can possibly be the product of human memory" (to quote N. M. Sarna of the Jewish Theological Seminary in Understanding Genesis).

8.23 Several updated studies of the Enumu Elish, such as The Babylonian Genesis by Alexander Heidel of the Oriental Institute, University of Chicago, have dwelt on the parallels in theme and structure between the Mesopotamian and biblical narratives. Both indeed *begin with the statement that refers to the primordial time when the Earth and "the heavens" (i.e. the asteroid belt) did not yet exist – i.e. to the time when Taimat orbited the sun.*

WHAT IS THE GENESIS STORY OF CREATION?

8.24 The Sumerian cosmology describes Taimat as a large watery planet orbiting between Mars and Jupiter prior to a cataclysmic close encounter with Nibiru, a planet with a highly irregular orbit. In recent decades, astronomers have detected a significant body is affecting the orbits of the known outer planets but we have yet to identify the cause. Tiamat was shattered by the gravitational stresses of the close encounter with Nibiru – with the greater part becoming our Earth and the remnants forming what we know as the Asteroid Belt.

8.25 The bible asserts that when the Earth was formed it was completely covered by water. If water was so abundant when Earth was created, then this strongly indicates that Tiamat was also a watery planet. The watery nature of Tiamat (aka Tehom) is mentioned in various biblical references. The prophet Isaiah (51:10) recalled "the primeval days" when the might of the Lord "carved the Haughty One, made spin the watery monster, drained off the waters of the mighty Tehom." Given most scholars believe this part of Isaiah, 'Deutero-Isaiah', was written during the Babylonian exile, the text appears to be clearly sourced from the Enuma Elish.

8.26 What was the "wind" of the Lord that "moved upon the face of the waters" of Tehom/Tiamat? In the Mesopotamian texts it is described as a moon of Nibiru. The texts vividly described the flashes and lightning strokes that burst off Nibiru as its orbit swung perilously close to Tiamat.

8.27 The continuing narrative of Genesis does not describe the ensuing splitting up of Tiamat or the breakup of her orbiting moons – described as 'winds' or 'helpers' in the Enuma Elish. It is evident, however, from the verse quoted above from Isaiah and from the narrative in Job (26:7-13), that the Hebrews were familiar with the skipped-over portions of the original description in the Enuma Elish.

8.28 English translations have removed the clarity of the Hebrew text of Job recalling how the *celestial Lord* smote "the helpers of the Haughty One," and he exalted the Lord who, having come from the outer reaches of space, cleaved Tiamat (Tehom) and measured out the Hammered Bracelet.

8.29 Two Hebrew words have been translated as 'heaven'. *Shama'im*, "the Heaven" – a name that in its first use in the Torah consists of the two words *sham* and *ma'im*, meaning literally "where the waters were". In the creation tale of Genesis, "the Heaven" was a specific celestial location, where Tiamat and her waters had been, and where after the collision the asteroid belt has been 'hammered out' – forming the *Raki'a* – generally translated as "Firmament" but literally meaning "Hammered-out Bracelet."

8.30 The astronomical knowledge of the ancient Sumerians, when first translated, was at variance with our conventional understanding and easily ascribed to myths relating to pagan gods. However, over the past century, changes in our scientific views and recent discoveries continue to validate details recorded by these ancient peoples at least 5,000 years ago. The Sumerians had explanations for the unique tilt of the earth and for our outsized Moon. They provided us with the concept of the 360° circle and the 12-part segmentation of the visible sky, giving the zodiac signs the names that we still use today. Indeed, the extent and source of their knowledge is deeply puzzling – for example, how could they know of Uranus (rediscovered in 1781) and Neptune (rediscovered in 1846)? Furthermore, they also knew the colour of these planets (pale blue and mid blue) – information we only "discovered" from pictures transmitted by Voyager 2 in 1989? Being a sceptic, I checked – the research by Sitchin, which included the Sumerian record of the colour of these planets, was published in 1976, in his work 'The Twelfth Planet'. Sitchin makes a detailed and fairly convincing case, certainly in the absence of any other explanation, that this knowledge was passed to the Sumerians by extra-terrestrial visitors – who, quite understandably, were regarded by Sumerians as gods.

A similar Islamic view drawn from the Qur'an

8.31 Islamic scholars have reached similar conclusions from examination of the same terms appearing in the Qur'an. One researcher, published an article 'Sama: The Hammered Bracelet' under a link that unfortunately no longer works so I summarise here the findings that the author noted. The articles stated that the Qur'an teaches there are seven asteroid belts, *sab'a samawat*. Sama is usually translated "heaven", so the astronomical implications of the verses referring to it are obscure. Some translators translate it as "cloud" because of the verses which say that Allah sent down water from the 'sama'. Today, we know that the asteroid belt is full of frozen water (ice).

8.32   The Arabic *'sama'* is the same as the Hebrew *'shamaim'*. The words are derived from the Akkadian *'rakkis'* which, it self, stems from the Sumerian *'rakia'*. The original Sumerian word, rakia, literally meant "hammered bracelet." It referred to the collection of celestial matter orbiting between Mars and Jupiter that is now referred to as the asteroid belt.

8.33   Genesis 1:8 states that the "hammered out bracelet" was named "heaven" (shamaim). While the Sumerians spoke of the asteroid belt as a bracelet, the Qur'an speaks of it as an adornment, a canopy that would be beautiful for those who beheld it. The Qur'an specifically says that the lower sama is adorned with lights, indicating that more asteroid belts, further out from the Sun, exist. Recently, a second asteroid belt has been discovered lying beyond Neptune. According to the Qur'an, there must be five more.

8.34   But how did the asteroid belt get there? Why is it a bunch of huge, broken rocks? As strange as it may seem, the Qur'an provides some clues. It says that the sama asteroid belt was once one body, but that Allah rent it asunder:- "Do not those who disbelieve see that the samawat (*asteroid belt*) and the earth were locked together (were one solid mass), so We rent them apart? And We made from water everything living." Sura 21:30.

8.35   So, the Qur'an very explicitly teaches the same as the Sumerian Enuma Elish – that planet Earth and the asteroid belt are both remnants of a larger planet which previously orbited between Mars and Jupiter. To this day, an Arabic word that's similar to Tiamat, Taammat, means "a calamity."

Garden of Eden – location and origin of the story

8.36   The setting of the story of the Garden of Eden pre-dates conventional history. In biblical terms it is linked to the first humans, Adam and Eve. It is therefore rather surprising that Genesis, where describing the flow of rivers in and out of Eden, is able to name the four rivers – and two remain common knowledge today – the Tigris and the Euphrates. This has led many to make assertions concerning the location of the Garden of Eden.

8.37   Recent advances in scanning technology and understanding of climate changes – combined with yet more translation errors – now provide us with a very plausible location and cultural explanation for what must have for a very long time been an oral tradition. Whilst I do not doubt such records exist, I have not found any reference to translated Sumerian tablets recording something similar to the biblical Garden of Eden story. That does not mean we will not find a Sumerian tale pre-dating the Genesis story of the Garden of Eden – as the vast majority of cuneiform tablets recovered have yet to be translated. Moreover, the names of the two rivers we instantly recognize and the fact that Abraham must have been familiar with the story mean it must have a Sumerian origin and a recorded version is awaiting discovery.

8.38 Let's start with location and the translation error which led to many weird location suggestions. Genesis 2:10 -14 provides strong location clues:

> [10] *And a river went out of Eden to water the garden; and from thence it was parted, and became into four heads.*
>
> [11] *The name of the first is Pison: that is it which compasseth the whole land of Havilah, where there is gold;*
>
> [12] *And the gold of that land is good: there is bdellium and the onyx stone.*
>
> [13] *And the name of the second river is Gihon: the same is it that compasseth the whole land of Ethiopia.*
>
> [14] *And the name of the third river is Hiddekel: that is it which goeth toward the east of Assyria. And the fourth river is Euphrates.*

8.39 The somewhat convoluted wording in Genesis that Eden's river "came into four heads" was explained by Biblical scholar and archaeologist Ephraim Speiser (1902 – 1965) who interpreted the text as referring to the four rivers upstream of their confluence merging into the one river watering the Garden. This is a strange perspective, but understandable if the description is of a folk memory, written millennia after the events concerned by those unfamiliar with the geography.

8.40 We recognize the Hiddekel is the Tigris but where now are the Pison and the Gihon? Theologians and historians have speculated the Garden being in almost as many places as Atlantis. Suggestions have included Mongolia, India and Ethiopia, some attempting links to other great rivers of the ancient world – the Nile and the Ganges. Others have focused on

WHAT IS THE GENESIS STORY OF CREATION?

Turkey because the headwaters of the Euphrates and the Tigris arise there as well as links in Genesis to Mount Ararat.

8.41 The identity of the Gihon, which "compasseth the whole land of Ethiopia", was for long a major problem. In Hebrew, the geographical reference was to "Gush" or "Kush". The translators of the King James Bible the rendered "Kush" as "Ethiopia" – confusing researchers for centuries. Dr. Juris Zarins, of Southwest Missouri State University, believes the Gihon is the Karun River, which rises in Iran and flows southwesterly toward the present Gulf. It was Ephraim Speiser who suggested that the mysterious Gush or Kush should be correctly written as Kashshu and that it refers to a people, then known as the Kashi or Galzu but nowadays known as the Kassites, who came from Elam, east of Babylon. After the Hittite king Mursilis I (c1556BC to c1526BC) attacked Babylon and destroyed the Hammurabi dynasty, the Hittites plundered it and left it defenseless – allowing the Kassites to take it over. The Kassites controlled Babylon until around 1155BC when they were defeated by the Assyrians. The remote bands of Israelites infiltrating from Edom and Moab towards the end of this period may have had knowledge of the Kassities but, as with most of Genesis, the knowledge was more likely gained from direct access to old tablets during the Exile in Babylon in the 6th Century BC. Today, the Karun is feeble and sickly from many dams and environmental abuse, entering the Euphrates at Khorramshahr – just before the current head of the Persian Gulf.

8.42 What of the fourth river, the Pison? This can be identified from references to the land of Havilah in the Table of Nations *(Genesis 10:7, 25:18)* as relating to localities and people within a Mesopotamian-Arabian framework. The Biblical evidence of Havilah is supported by LANDSAT images from space. These images clearly show a "fossil river" that once flowed through northern Arabia and through the now dry beds, which are known today as the Wadi Riniah and the Wadi Batin. Finally, Genesis identifies this region through which the Pison flowed was rich in bdellium, an aromatic gum resin, that can still be found in north Arabia, and gold, which was still mined in the general area in the 1950s. The Pison would have joined the Euphrates somewhere near Basra, just before the Karun.

8.43 So, we now have good reason to believe we have identified the four rivers that flowed into the Garden of Eden – but it suggests the Garden itself is

PART ONE: GOD, ENKI, RA/MARDUK & YAHWEH

now underwater – maybe the area at the head of the Persian Gulf. This makes absolute sense as the description of a verdant bountiful Garden suggests a lowland area benefiting from abundant fresh water.

8.44 Dr Juris Zarins first published his work on locating the Garden of Eden in 1983 and Dora Jane Hamblin published a very good descriptive article of his work in 1986 entitled *Has the Garden of Eden been located at last?* Dr Zarins identified ancient changes in climate as the likely cause of social changes in the region which led to the displacement of early hunter gatherer communities from flooded areas and shifts from prevailing hunter gather lifestyles to domestication of animals and cultivation of crops. Dr Zarins mapped the coastline of the Persian Gulf showing that 30,000 years ago the head of the Gulf was near the Straits of Hormuz – almost 1,000km downstream of the present position. Around 15,000BC climatic changes significantly reduced rainfall and the land may have become relatively arid. Low rainfall persisted until around 6,000BC when far moister climate, known as the Neolithic Wet Phase, would have replenished the rivers and the low lying areas again – restoring a lush paradise for hunter gatherers. By 6,000BC it is estimated that the Persian Gulf headwaters had risen to within 150km of the present coastline – pinpointing the most likely area for the Garden of Eden.

8.45 New knowledge emerging over the past 50 years may have refined the climate data. We know the last ice age maxima was c24000 years ago with the three dramatic climate change phases referred to as the Oldest, Older and Younger Dryas Periods. Sea levels generally rose throughout the period since the last ice age maxima – but rose faster at certain times. As covered in the Prequel, sea levels rose very fast immediately after the Hiawatha meteor impact in 10,765BC in western Greenland. We also know this rapid rise in sea levels, following the huge loss of ice slowed again after 9,600BC. We also know that rapid changes led to the introduction of crop cultivation and the domestication of animals in the Fertile Crescent very soon afterwards.

8.46 Taking Dr Zairns' work together with the more recent climate data – corroborates his theory, if slightly modifying the dates. Critically, it depends how the current area of the Persian Gulf that was underwater shrunk between 9,600BC and the 6,000BC date Dr Zarin gives for the return of high rainfall and lush vegetation. The return of lush conditions in the Persian Gulf area would have enabled the hunter gatherer

WHAT IS THE GENESIS STORY OF CREATION?

community to flourish. Sumerian records have been found which tell of a luxuriant and lovely land they called Dilmun. On the adjacent higher land around the Gulf – the Havilah/Sinai area of northern Arabia to the west and the Tigris/Euphrates valley to the north – agriculture may have developed using the crops developed over the preceding few millennia in the Zagros foothills. These new farmers are known as the Ubaid people, as proto-Sumerian culture dating around c5,300BC to c4,100BC – see section 5.11 above.

8.47 We also know from Sumerian records that the demise of Sumeria was partly caused by the steady inundation of its most fertile lands by encroaching salt water as sea levels rose at the end of the 2nd millennium. BC. This implies crop cultivation had spread into the very fertile Gulf lowlands, maybe into the margins of the Garden of Eden. Thus pressure on the hunter gatherers domain came from both directions – cultivating farmers encroaching from the north west and the rising sea levels from the south east. During the period from 8,000BC and 4,000BC, slowly but continuously, the rising level of the Persian Gulf submerged the low lying Garden of Eden. This forced the hunter gatherer community to move on – pitting the survivors against the settled farming communities. We have found evidence of Ubaid communities along the western coast of the Gulf down past Kuwait – exactly the areas that retreating hunter gatherers fleeing from the Garden of Eden would naturally migrate to. Faced with more technically advanced communities, those fleeing from the Garden of Eden realised that their days of leisure were over and henceforth food came only from working the land, from the sweat of their brows. This was the punishment for their sins, as recorded in Genesis.

8.48 Recent work by geologists has established an event which may have also had an influence on the story of the expulsion from the Garden of Eden. A meteor impact in the Indian Ocean named after one of the researchers who first postulated its location – Professor Lloyd Burckle of Columbia University. Evidence of the damage caused by the resulting tsunami on the surrounding coastlines of India, Africa and Australia helped pinpoint the location of the impact site and the height of the resulting tsunami – estimated at 300m. Whilst the hooked shape of the Persian Gulf would to some extent have reduced the impact force, the fertile delta of the confluence of the Tigris and Euphrates south of modern Basra would have been devasted – a seminal event in the history of the local people.

The Holocene Impact Working Group (HIWG) which is looking at potential linkages between impacts and the climate oscillations of the three Dryas periods gives a date range for the Burckle impact of 3000BC to 2800BC. Another researcher and author, Kevin Curran, in his work Fall of a Thousand Suns: How near misses and comet impacts affected the religious beliefs of our ancestors , identifies a specific date of 3067BC – his book is a very interesting read.

8.49   It is interesting to compare the creation story of Judaism with other creation stories. Most such belief systems either credit god or small teams of visiting wise men (such as the Seven Apkallu) – with teaching humans how to cultivate crops, how to make bread and beer, identify medicinal properties, weave textiles, construct buildings, etc.. Genesis describes a hunter gatherer society and includes a weak excuse (eating a fruit) to shove them into farming. A set of clothes is made for them but there is no record of any teaching. Given the overwhelming evidence that Genesis was crafted from older creation stories, this is a strange omission – see also paragraph 3.5 above. But maybe it also points to the young age of Genesis, its writers could not image a time when humans did not know how to farm, to cook, identify natural medicines, etc. and saw no role for god in how these skills were gained.

8.50   I'll close this section by referring to recent research identifying some intriguing translation errors underlying well-known but rather odd phrases from Genesis – namely that Adam was formed from *clay* and Eve was formed from taking one of Adam's *ribs*. From this, Genesis suggests the first man and women were made as mature adults – which seems bizarre!

The lingua franca at the time of the exile from Judah was Akkadian but for scientific and religious matters the use of Sumerian was retained. The two languages were similar but there were many differences, the Babylonian astronomer-priests faithfully maintained the original Sumerian star tables and eclipse records in that language.

Nebuchadnezzar's library, where the top craftsmen from Judah were based, would certainly have held multiple copies of the Enuma Elish in the original Sumerian language. (NB the Babylonians substituted the name of their national god, Marduk, for the original name of the highly elliptical planet Nibiru). So, the explanation, for clay and rib may be revealed:

- » Babylonian word Tît (potters clay) and in Hebrew tit meaning 'mud', being confused with the Sumerian word 'Tî-it' – meaning that source of life, i.e. a seed or an egg.

- » Babylonian ti (rib) confused with the Sumerian Tî – meaning to create life.

These fundamental translation errors clearly reveal to us the period when most of the Pentateuch was written. This further reinforces arguments that (i) the Enuma Elish and other Sumerian historical records were a major source of the Torah, and (ii) indicates authorship of Genesis was mainly in Babylon, between say 580BC and 540BC.

9

Who was Abraham?

9.1 The historical existence of Abraham has been validated by records found on numerous clay tablets unearthed in Ur with surprising explanations now being found to illuminate some of the incongruous details given in Genesis.

9.2 Sarah, Abraham's wife was his half-sister, the daughter of Terah his father and Tohwait (Nfry-ta-Tjenen) the former wife of a deceased Pharaoh, Amenemhat I. This now provides some explanations:

    (i)   Sarah's original name, Sarai – meaning Princess;

    (ii)   Sarai having an Egyptian handmaiden, Hagar – with whom Abraham fathered Ishmael;

    (iii)   Why, upon entering Egypt, Abraham and his family were welcomed and given hospitality by none other than the Pharaoh, Senusret I, who was half-brother to Abraham's wife;

    (iv)   Why Abraham introduced his wife as his sister – in those times culturally a more senior title than a mere wife. Offspring from a union with a sister (by another mother) took precedence over all other issue in inheriting from their father;

    (v)   Why Pharaoh Senusret was interested in Sarai, his half-sister, who could help preserve his bloodline and provide an eligible successor

PART ONE: GOD, ENKI, RA/MARDUK & YAHWEH

to maintain his Dynasty.

9.3 From cuneiform tablets recovered from excavations in Ur, it is clear that Abraham's family held prominent positions – his father was governor of the province surrounding Ur, the capital of Sumeria at that time. Citations have been found for Abraham's four preceding male ancestors as noted in Genesis: Terah, Nahor, Serug, and Pelug – who were provincial governors and commissioners. Peleg's father, Eber is suggested by Zecharia Sitchin in *The Wars of Gods and Men* as the origin of the term 'Ibri', translated as 'Hebrew'. By identifying Abraham and his family as Ibri, the suffix 'i' denotes 'a native of', and 'Ibr', a root word meaning 'crossing' which corresponds with the Akkadian name for the city of Nippur which stood at the crossroads of two ancient highways. So Ibri might just mean a native of the city of Nippur. Nippur was a sacred city with a major palace dedicated to Enlil, the Lord Most High, known to the Israelites as El Elyon. In ancient culture, religious leadership was synonymous with political leadership, the name 'Terah' actually denotes an 'oracle priest', the priest that the god spoke to, i.e. the high priest. The family move from Nippur to Ur might be connected with the delegation of rulership of Mesopotamia from Enlil to his son Nannar (Sin in Akkadian) and the re-establishment of Ur as the capital of Sumeria (known as the 3rd Dynasty of Ur), c2120BC. Both Ur and Harran (the northern capital) were longstanding cult centres for Nannar.

9.4 However, whilst the 3rd Dynasty of Ur established control over an area similar to modern day Iraq, its rule was short lived. Records show Ur faced three major problems (i) rising sea levels in the Persian Gulf, causing salinity which ruined its major arable lands – see paragraph 8.47 above; (ii) attacks from nearby Elam (nowadays Iran) against weak kings which led to military defeat and the end of Sumeria – between 2004BC and 1960BC; and, (iii) the complete devastation of Ur and the entire surrounding area dated to 1960BC. This last devastation is recorded in the Lamentation tablets which seem to describe something far worse than a military defeat using bronze armour and weapons. One text states: *"Ur is destroyed, bitter is its lament. The country's blood now fills its holes like hot bronze in a mold. Bodies dissolve like fat in the sun. Our temple is destroyed. The gods have abandoned us like migrating birds. Smoke lies on our cities like a shroud."* The full text has been published by the Oriental Institute of the University of Chicago (oi.uchicago.edu) entitled *"Lamentation over the destruction of Ur"*. The overall impression is of destruction by an 'evil wind' and great storm which killed almost all people and livestock. The text lists all the gods (maybe the elite human rulers – see the Prequel to this series) abandoning their palace temples and devastation of all the farms. Some have speculated that the timing equates to the biblical destruction of Sodom and Gomorrah, which both Genesis and archaeological evidence indicates might have been caused by a massive explosion – a meteorite impact or a nuclear bomb with maybe fallout affecting southern Sumeria. Toxic winds might have been caused by a meteorite and certainly by a nuclear explosion, which would account for the evil winds and deaths of all livestock – which does not suggest contemporary military action.

9.5 Abraham's father, Terah, had (at least) two wives – Tohwait (mother of Sarai) and Yawnu (mother of Abraham). Jewish sources including the Midrash and texts from the Dead Sea Scrolls identify Tohwait as Nfry-ta-Tjewnen, the former wife of Pharaoh Amenemhat I. Her son by this marriage was the next pharaoh, Senusret I. This meant Sarai was Senusret's maternal half-sister as well as Abraham's paternal half-sister. Senusret, recognizing Sarai as his half-sister, would have leapt at the chance to maintain the highest purity for his blood line. It was standard practice for pharaohs to marry their half-sisters to progress the kingship through the female line. Genesis 12:18-19 enigmatically records the pharaoh saying to Abraham "what have you done to me? Why did you not tell me she is your wife? Why did you say, 'she is my sister' ***so that I took her to be my wife?***

9.6 Genesis 20:2 retells the meeting of Abraham with the Egyptian king, where Abraham again states that Sarah "is my sister" but omits to say she is also his wife. This time God, or at least El Elyon (the initial god named in Genesis) intervenes to tell the king he was "*but* a dead man, for the woman which thou hast taken; for she *is* a man's wife." The king then claims that he "had not come near her...". This strikes me as a rather peculiar exchange - why would God bother to tell the Pharaoh that he had slept with another man's wife – and why would a Pharaoh bother to deny it? This sounds more like the plot from a soap opera!

9.7 This opens up a major issue. Non biblical Hebrew sources indicate the they were married for a while – ***so was Isaac the son of Sarai and Pharaoh Senusret?*** Genesis indicates Abraham and his entourage stayed in Egypt for some years – certainly time for the famine to pass and for his entourage to swell considerably in size. Whilst Genesis brands

Sarai as barren, it is more likely that the trouble lay with Abraham, it also records the pharaoh's advisors telling him that Sarai was extremely attractive. If Isaac was the son of Pharaoh Senusret, then the seemingly enigmatic details of the covenant would fall very neatly into place. The prophesy of lands to be ruled by the seed of Abraham and Sarai in Genesis 15:19-21 (rather extravagantly prophesying ruling over the lands of the Hittites, modern Turkey, and east as far as the River Euphrates) partly came true for Sarai's bloodline (whether through her mother or through her liaison with Senusret) the Egyptian pharaohs but never for Abraham's offspring. If Isaac was not Abraham's son it would also explain why Genesis has God asking Abraham to sacrifice his ***only*** son, at that stage, which would be Ishmael – which is the case stated in the Quran. Isaac may have been a name given to one of Abraham's later sons.

9.8   The account in Genesis blames Sarai for Abraham's failure to produce offspring but knowing her husband had been promised the post of founding patriarch for a great nation, Sarai presented Abraham with her Egyptian handmaiden, Hagar, 'to be his wife'. This sounds rather quaint considering Abraham was a wealthy tribal patriarch, twice recorded as having been given 'many male and female slaves' by other friendly rulers. However, once Hagar conceives, she is chastised and banished by Sarai (Genesis 16:1-16), as if the outcome was unexpected. After Ishmael, the first son of Abraham, is born to Hagar, it is then announced in Genesis 17 that his inheritance is to be superseded by a forthcoming son of Sarai – a son who will be named Isaac. This also indicates late authorship, so late that the Israelites had forgotten Egyptian rules of inheritance. For Abraham, the issue of Sarai, being his half-sister, took precedence over the first born from Hagar – whether or not she was his wife.

9.9   If Isaac was indeed Abraham's son, then the terms of the covenant in Genesis 15:18-19 would have taken longer to be fulfilled – with Akhenaten (possibly a role model for Moses – see section 10). Akhenaten, whose mother was a descendant of Isaac, became pharaoh when the Egyptian empire was near its zenith.

9.10 All of this paints a rather different picture of Abraham than traditionally portrayed. Abraham appears not as an everyday nomad, but as a wealthy ruler with gold, silver, camels, herds and a large household of servants. This fits rather better with his earlier brief portrayal as a military commander (Genesis 14) who defeated the armies of four kings to rescue his nephew Lot.

9.11 As the scion of a powerful ruling dynasty in Ur, the capital province of the Sumerian Empire, Abraham would have benefitted from the extensive Sumerian education system. The principal gods that Abraham would have been brought up to know and acknowledge would have been Enlil, as supreme (who became El Elyon in Canaanite records predating Abraham's arrival in Haran), and Nannar the chief city deity (aka Sin in Akkadian and represented by the crescent Moon). Accordingly, in Genesis 12, where Abraham is told to go forth from his father's house to new lands, the instruction is merely attributed to "the Lord", but in Hebrew written as "El Elyon". Thus, Abraham is instructed by the same god he has habitually worshipped all his life. Everything suggests that the same old lifelong pagan god Abraham had always worshipped – had given him this new instruction. If Abraham had suddenly been confronted by God, the Creator of the Universe, this mind shattering event would surely be described slightly differently. Alternatively, if Abraham had always worshipped the true Creator, then we need to seriously re-evaluate El Elyon/ Enlil and the whole Sumerian pantheon of gods that have been denigrated as pagan gods.

10

Israelites: in bondage or enslaving the Egyptians?

10.1 The story of Moses tells of Joseph's descendants falling into bondage and eventually after hundreds of years being rescued by God acting through Moses to persuade the Pharaoh to let the Israelites depart.

10.2 The description given in Exodus and Numbers is challenging to believe as factually true. Many explain away all questions as requiring faith to believe in numerous miracles. However, if miracles had occurred which explain the miraculous events then one would assume other non-miraculous details to be factually accurate.

10.3 However, if a historian looks at the Exodus it seems to contain many examples like the spoof verse Exodus 40:39 quoted in the introduction (1.45) of this book.

10.4 The history of Egypt in the first half of the second millennium BC is now reasonably well understood, it included waves of migrating people from Canaan who ruled parts of Egypt for around 110 years. From what we now know of these Canaanites, whom the Egyptians called the Hyksos, suggests that they came from the right locality (Canaan) at the right time – with successive waves migrating into Egypt from c1800BC. During a period of Egyptian dynastic weakness, the Hyksos seized control of Lower Egypt which they ruled from Avaris between 1655BC and 1545BC. During this period, there is evidence of crop failures occurring which might have formed the basis of some of the memories of famines recorded in biblical texts. Crop failures might have been due to climatic variation but would not have been helped by Hyksos herdsmen (known as the shepherd kings) disrupting and displacing crop cultivating Egyptians. However, it is clear that the Canaanites were the rulers not the slaves and that the Egyptians eventually defeated them and chased them out of Egypt.

10.5   Somewhere during the reign of Amenemhat IV (c1800BC), the penultimate king of the 12th Dynasty, the regular expeditions to the copper and turquoise mines of what is now called Sinai came to an end. At about the same time, the archaeological record shows that a man of obvious foreign origin, usurped royal power and controlled at least part of the Nile Delta. He was succeeded by a long list of foreign kings, whose control never seems to have extended beyond Lower Egypt, who are grouped in the 14th Dynasty, which ruled from the city of Avaris. The circumstances under which a foreigner was able to seize power over a prosperous region in the country, are not known. Perhaps Amenemhat IV's non-royal parentage caused some dynastic feud with the remaining members of the old royal family, weakening the position of the central government. The fact that Amenemhat IV's immediate successor, Nefrusobek, was not one of his surviving sons, but a daughter of Amenemhat III, may have been an ultimate attempt of the members of the 12th Dynasty to hold on to power. That this attempt failed, is shown by the fact that Nefrusobek's successor, Sebekhotep I, was the son of Amenemhat IV. Sebekhotep I is considered to be the founder of the 13th Dynasty, which ruled Upper-Egypt, while the 14th Dynasty held power over Lower Egypt. It seems that any initial hostilities between the Upper and the Lower Egyptian Dynasties soon ended as records show the kings of the 13th Dynasty were able to trade with the Levant, while the 14th Dynasty could trade with Nubia, each dynasty thus allowing the other safe passage on its trading routes.

10.6   Despite the initial rivalry and the kings of the 13th Dynasty still officially claiming kingship over the entire country, the first halves of both concurrent dynasties appear to have been fairly stable. The second part of the 13th Dynasty, however, was marked by usurpations and kings openly proclaiming they were commoners not royalty. The last kings of the two dynasties followed each other in rapid succession, which drastically weakened the authority of their governments. Remarkably, several kings of the second half of the 14th Dynasty, had the word 'nourishment' as part of their royal names, an indication that the provisions of food become

ISRAELITES: IN BONDAGE OR ENSLAVING THE EGYPTIANS?

a topic of high political importance. At the same time, burials in Avaris, the capital of the 14th Dynasty, often lacked the usual food offerings and have the character of quick mass interments. All of this appears to point towards famines ravaging the habitually very fertile Nile Delta. The results of these famines may have been felt throughout the entire country. Not only may there have been a general lack of food in the whole of Egypt, but famines quite often resulted in plagues which explain the quick succession of kings in both Dynasties. Perhaps the memory of famine and plagues in this period became a folk memory of the Hyksos people.

10.7 As a result of the weakened positions of the 13th and 14th Dynasties, Egypt lay open to outside aggression. Around 1660BC, Egypt was invaded by a group of Canaanites, whose leader used the title *HqA-xAs.wt*, 'ruler of the foreign land', or Hyksos. The Hyksos easily conquered Avaris as well as Memphis, causing the end of both the 13th and 14th Dynasty and founding their own dynasty, the 15th Dynasty. The fall of the 13th Dynasty created a power vacuum in the southern part of Upper Egypt, which was quickly filled by two local dynasties: one in Abydos and one in Thebes, the latter's power extending from Thebes to Aswan in the South. The kings of the Theban dynasty are grouped in the 16th Dynasty. At the same time, the Hyksos pressed on further to the south, and after it had been independent for about 20 years, they made an end to the Abydene Dynasty. It would take them another 30 years before they would successfully end the 16th Dynasty based in Thebes, thereby gaining control over the entire country.

10.8 The Hyksos kings, however, were not able to maintain their control over the whole of Egypt, and only a few years after it had been conquered, Thebes again arose as an independent state, and home to the 17th Dynasty. The circumstances that led to Thebes' renewed independence are not clear. A change of power in the 15th Dynasty may hint at some dynastic troubles among the Hyksos, and it is possible that the Thebans took advantage of the situation not only to reclaim their autonomy but also to extend their rule as far north as Abydos. After the Theban conquest of Abydos, a status quo appears to have been established between the 15th and 17th Dynasty and both dynasties even appear to have entered into trade. This situation lasted at least until the reign of Seqenenre, the penultimate king of the 17th Dynasty, during which hostilities between the Thebans and the Hyksos appear to have been reignited. A story relates a quarrel between Seqenenre and Apophis, the penultimate king of the 15th Dynasty. The historicity of this story can, of course, be doubted, but the mummy of Seqenenre shows signs of a violent death, consistent with the weapons the Hyksos used.

10.9   The first historically recorded traces of a war against the Hyksos are dated to the reign of Seqenenre's successor, Kamose. Two stelae commemorate Kamose's struggle against the Hyksos and their vassals. Against the advice of his council, Kamose continued the war, punishing all those who had collaborated with the foreigners. But, it was Kamose's successor, Ahmose, who would finally succeed in overthrowing and evicting the Hyksos from Egypt. The exact dating of this eviction is disputed but most assess this to have been around 1550BC.

10.10 There are many references in Exodus that suggest that those accompanying Moses into exile may not have been slaves after all. Special rules are mentioned for the Passover meal to decide how to include the *slaves* of the Israelites; when departing the Israelites took large quantities of gold and silver, apparently *given* to them by Egyptians happy to see them depart; upon reaching Sinai and finding water scarce in the desert, the Israelites complained that they were better off in Egypt where they had pots of meat and as much food as they could eat – which seems inconsistent with the tale of abject slavery from which they were supposedly delivered?

10.11 The Egyptian records suggest many successive waves of Hyksos immigrants and also a number of different waves of emigration during their departure but the main exodus would probably have followed the defeat of Khamudi by Pharaoh Ahmose c1550BC.

Key problems with the story of the Exodus as told in the Torah

10.12 If read carefully, the plagues overlap, for example killing off cattle after they have already been slaughtered by a preceding plague. Taken at face value, the plagues would have utterly destroyed Egypt, its people and its entire agricultural resources, the land would be devoid of animals and vegetation – yet there is no mention of any such calamity in either Egyptian records, which are seamless throughout the range of postulated dates for Moses, nor in any other contemporary cultures – many of which traded extensively with Egypt and would have surely noticed Egypt being all but entirely wiped out?

ISRAELITES: IN BONDAGE OR ENSLAVING THE EGYPTIANS?

10.13   The Plagues and Passover include many odd features – why would God take so much effort to repeatedly harden Pharaoh's heart? This God can identify which cattle belong to Egyptians and which belong to Israelites – but cannot identify which people are which – requiring blood to be painted on door lintels? And, if all the Egyptian first born were killed – presumably under inheritance law, the Pharaoh himself would have been a first born – but he was missed out?

10.14   The logistic requirements to assemble the Israelites ready for the Exodus defy rational analysis. According to Numbers 1:46, the Israelites comprised 603,550 able bodied men. Given the large family sizes in those days and the average age of some developing countries today being around 20, the total host would have been around 4 times that – some 2.4 million. Think how long it takes for 50,000 people to march from Causeway Bay to Tamar each June 4th – and they don't have enormous flocks of sheep, goats, etc. and wagons laden with gold and silver – plus a minimum of say 250,000 tents (10 to a tent?), tents which were miraculously collected at short notice.

10.15   The vast host of around 2.4 million is impossibly large to contemplate venturing into Sinai. It is reasonable to assume the great majority moved on foot. If the multitude marched 10 abreast and allowing 1 metre separation between each rank, the file would stretc.h over 240 km – and that's without the herds of sheep, goats, and wagons loaded with gold, silver and hundreds of thousands of tents. Even if they moved 40 abreast, which if you think about it, would be fiendishly difficult, the line would still be 60km in length plus the flocks, wagons, etc..

10.16   According to estimates, the total population of Egypt rose from around 1 million in 3000BC, to around 2 million in 2000BC, to 3 million in 1000BC and reached 5 million at the time of the Roman invasion (see: reshfim.com). These estimates suggest the exodus removed a number equal to the then total population of Egypt!! If Joseph's extended family had been 70 going into Egypt, then an exodus of 2,400,000 people after even 400 years would suggest an astonishing reproductive rate.

10.17   Another calibration is the context in Babylon, where the bulk of the Torah was written, trying to portray the Israelites as a worthy people of equal stature to other major powers and able to smite all its enemies (so long as Yahweh was onside). The idea that the Israelites could field an army just exceeding 600,000 may be related to the belief at that time that Cyrus fielded an army 600,000 strong when attacking Babylon (Charles Rollin, *The Ancient History of the Egyptians, Carthaginians, Assyrians, Babylonians, Medes, Persians, Macedonians and Grecians*, 1852). Others have indicated that the Hebrew word 'eleph' translated as 'thousand', also connotes 'group' or 'troops' suggesting the possibility of a far smaller exodus of 2 to 3 thousand people. The 600,000 number has taken on many mystical meanings for the Hebrews – in the Kabbalah there are 600,000 letters, aspects and interpretations of the Torah; mystical Judaism has 600,000 Souls, etc..

10.18 Consideration of Numbers chapters 1 to 3 makes most peoples' eyes glaze over but certain of the figures reveal obvious errors and very late authorship. Numbers is generally believed to have been written mainly by the Priestly source in Babylon during the Exile. One fact that supports this is Numbers 3:47 which explains the 'sanctuary shekel' weighs 20 'gerahs' – according to the Jewish Encyclopaedia the term 'gerah' was only used during the Babylonian exile. The main focus at the start of Numbers is to emphasise the size (and by implication the strength) of the Israelite army and the temporary establishment of some history for the 12 tribes. However, the figures do not add up! In Numbers 3:39 the total Levite males over one month old are recorded as 22,000, whilst the total first born males of the non-Levite tribes is stated as 22,273 – justifying the collection by Aaron of 5 shekels times 273 souls. However, the statement that there are 22,273 first born males undermines the purported numbers of all the tribes. It suggests the average (non-Levite) Israelite mother had produced over 100 children – 603,550 fit adult males aged over 20 plus a similar number of males under 20 and other males over 20 but unfit for the army, doubled to include a similar number of females. So, a population of around 2.4 million contained only 22,273 first-born males – which suggests an astonishing fecundity of 108 per female!!! And, these were the survivors – one would expect high rates of infant mortality at this time – which would raise the number of children per female far higher.

10.19 The huge volume of animal sacrifices supposedly made during 40 years in Sinai desert would have required a good supply of firewood and consumed huge flocks, requiring vast acreages of verdant pasture to sustain them. The showbread required to be made from finest quality wheat flour and virgin olive oil would also have provided quite a challenge to

ISRAELITES: IN BONDAGE OR ENSLAVING THE EGYPTIANS?

source in the desert.

10.20 A huge host, including 600,000 soldiers, plus their wives, children and elders, lived on wafers of Manna for 40 years whilst vast flocks of sheep and oxen, and thousands of birds were regularly sacrificed as burnt offerings, with piles of "showbread made from the finest wheat flour" (Exodus 29.2). It seems unlikely that a huge army would happily reserve such flocks solely for godly sacrifice and tolerate consumption being reserved for the Levite priests.

10.21 In Numbers 7:12 to 83, the heads of each of the twelve tribes each brought offerings of "one silver plate weighing 130 shekels (c1.5kg), one silver sprinkling bowl weighing 70 shekels (c0.8kg), one gold dish weighing 10 shekels", plus identical quantities of assorted flour, oil and animals. Numbers 12:85 even confirms that each silver and gold vessel presented weighed exactly the same – suggesting some kind of smelting furnaces had been set up in the Sinai desert, fuelled by what? And, a production line to fashion standard vessels of identical weight.

10.22 An interesting alternative calculation of the duration in Egypt (400 years per Genesis 15:13, although 430 years per Exodus 12:40 – different authors?) is available on a Jewish website (chabad.org), which states:

> Our sages explain that the countdown of 400 years began with Isaac's birth. God's promise does not refer to Egypt by name, rather to a "land that is not theirs." As soon as Abraham had a child, his seed were subjected to living in lands that were not theirs – including Canaan, which wasn't "theirs" at the time.
>
> Isaac was sixty years old when Jacob was born, and Jacob was 130 years old when he went down to Egypt. This means that 190 of the 400 years elapsed before the Israelites arrived in Egypt. So, the Israelites were in Egypt for only 210 years.
>
> Interestingly, when Jacob first instructed his sons to descend to Egypt, he said, "Go down ("ורדו") there and buy food." The numerical value of the Hebrew letters of the word "ורדו" ("*redu*," "go down") is exactly 210!
>
> A period of 210 years would also fit better the period of Hyksos domination of Lower Egypt.

11

Who was Moses?

11.1   Given the amazing exploits recorded in Exodus, it is very surprising that there is so little reference to Moses in the subsequent books of the OT and none whosoever in any of the records of the Egyptians or indeed of any culture. This is despite our having recovered hundreds of thousands of original clay tablets from various cities contemporaneous with the period in which Moses and the Exodus are supposed to have occurred. Psalm 78, which is believed to date from the end of King David's reign (c1015BC) reads like the executive summary of the Exodus and may have provided the genesis for the much of the story of Moses. Psalm 78 makes around 100 references to El Shaddai (an alternative name for El Elyon, the name of God prior to the Burning Bush incident), names Yahweh only twice, Jacob twice and Joseph once – but the supposed star of the whole story, Moses, is glaringly absent!! How could David have written a Psalm with 72 verses describing the whole Exodus and forgotten about Moses? The obvious conclusion is that 'Moses' had not yet been invented in David's time (c1000BC) – Moses was an embellishment added to the story during the Babylonian Exile (597BC to 538BC).

11.2   "We cannot be sure that Moses ever lived because there are no traces of his earthly existence outside of tradition" – states Egyptologist Dr. Jan Assmann, in *Moses the Egyptian*. Of the other patriarchs, e.g. Abraham and Joseph, we do have substantial evidence, as set out elsewhere in this booklet.

11.3   Moses appears to be a composite character woven from a rich variety of

PART ONE: GOD, ENKI, RA/MARDUK & YAHWEH

oral traditions and myths.

11.4 If the Israelites were really the Hyksos and their release was in reality closer to an expulsion, then where did the Moses story come from? Perhaps, as some have postulated over the past few hundred years, the original model for Moses was the Pharaoh Akhenaten. Intriguingly, this Pharaoh, a descendant of Joseph, had an Israelite mother and when ascending the throne, introduced Aten as a monotheistic god for Egypt, without any image and represented only by the rays of the sun. His version of monotheism differs starkly from the Israelite idea of Yahweh – most strikingly Aten was held to be the sole god for all peoples – not just Egyptians. In contrast, the Israelites were very clear that Yahweh was theirs alone and that they alone were the chosen people of Yahweh. And, it is clear from the Torah that the Israelites believed that other peoples had their own gods and that gods were linked to territorial areas.

The two Joseph's and the father to a Pharaoh

11.5 The Torah records El Elyon's promise to Joseph that his seed would rule the Egyptian empire (Genesis 45:8). Likewise Abraham had been promised that his seed would rule from the River of Egypt to the River Euphrates (Genesis 15:18-21). For many centuries the Egyptians did rule over most of the area between these two rivers but Abraham's seed never did – unless it refers to the issue of Amenhotep III and Tiye (see 11.11). The promise in Genesis 15:18-21 specifies overlordship over both Hittites (who first appeared over the Caucasus mountains a few hundred years after Abraham, occupying modern Turkey) and the Amorites – who also emerged after Abraham, creating the first Babylonian Empire based at Babylon. Again, fulfilment could be from the issue of Amenhotep and Tiye as the Egyptians did occupy part of Turkey for a while and even sailed a fleet on the Euphrates. But for the Israelites this promise is clearly anachronistic and its prophesy clearly failed as the Israelites never occupied any lands of the Amorites or the Hittites.

11.6 El Shaddai as a name for God appears frequently in Hebrew scripture, mostly in Genesis and Psalm 78 – the conventional English translation being 'God Almighty'. The derivation of Shaddai is disputed – El Shaddai has been tentatively identified with the šedim (שדים) of Deuteronomy 32:17 and Psalm 106:37-38, a Canaanite deity. (Could šedim be the Canaanite name for the god called Sin in Akkadian?). According to Ernst

Knauf, a professor of Israelite history at Bern University, "El Shaddai" means "God of the Wilderness" and originally would not have had a doubled "d" but originally would have been "śaday" with the sound "šin" related to the word "śadé" meaning "the (uncultivated) field", Another theory is that Shaddai is a derivation of a Semitic stem that appears in the Akkadian shadû ("mountain") and shaddā`û or shaddû`a ("mountain-dweller"), one of the names of Amurru a small Amorite enclave north of present day Lebanon which switched allegiance back and forth between the Egyptian and Hittite kingdoms. It is intriguing that these ideas are also suggestive of Yahweh being placed in a mountainous wilderness in the land of Sin, i.e. in Northern Arabia. Perhaps the three gods El Shaddai, Sin and Yahweh were all one and the same?

11.7 When I was a schoolboy, I read with great interest the arguments over the dating of the Exodus, the apparent 400 odd years either duplicated or missed out, particularly Velikovsky's book *Ages in Chaos*. Although, a huge volume of new historical information has come to light over the 60+ years since that book was written, it did highlight some problems in the conventional record of history. The problems seem to have stemmed from scholars in the 18th and 19th centuries, faced with Egyptian records which only listed Pharaohs reigns in terms of durations rather than dates which could be linked to anything, and knowing sometimes they included co-rulers, deciding to rely on the Old Testament – as a seemingly coherent record of the period from Abraham to the Babylonian Captivity. This led to the conventional dating of the Egyptian Pharaohs to be based largely on Bishop Ussher's simplistic calculations – that Jacob moved his extended family to Egypt in 1706BC and the Exodus took place in 1491BC. Fortunately, much has been unearthed and translated in the past few decades – hundreds of references in original clay tablets to contemporaneous Pharaohs by Sumerian, Akkadian and Babylonian kings whose dates have been corroborated extensively.

11.8 A good example of the time gap is Moses father-in-law, named in Exodus 2.18-21 as Reuel, whereas by Exodus 3.1 the name of the father-in-law has changed to Jethro. This suggests that the compilers of the Torah skipped c400 years of history by leaping from Reuel, son of Esau (Genesis 36.4) to his descendant, Jethro, Lord of Midian, many generations later.

11.9 If Genesis is read carefully, Jacob's son Joseph, who was sold into captivity, does not appear to be the same Joseph that rose to be vizier of Egypt. Jacob's son requested his bones be returned to Canaan for burial whilst the vizier Joseph was embalmed and buried in Egypt (Genesis 50.26). When the Israelites left Egypt during the Exodus, Moses took Joseph's bones with him (Exodus 13:19). These bones were buried at Shechem, in the parcel of ground that Jacob bought from the sons of Hamor (Joshua 24:32). However, Joseph, the prime minister, was embalmed and his embalmed body can now be seen, together with that of his wife, Tuya, in the Cairo Museum!!

11.10 Joseph is quoted as saying "God has made me a father to a Pharaoh" (Genesis 45.8) an impressive statement for someone sold into slavery. Such a prophesy only makes sense if the compilers of Genesis knew that one of his descendants had in fact become ruler of Egypt. Long after Jacob migrated to Egypt, there was an Egyptian vizier named Jusuf (Yuya), the principal minister to Thutmose IV (1413 to 1405BC) and to his son, Amenhotep III (1405 to 1367BC). His tomb, sited in the Valley of the Kings caused great surprise as no one outside immediate royal families had been discovered there. Such tombs always show inscriptions of the god under whose protection the occupant was placed – usually Ra (later AmenRa), Ptah or Seth – but Jusuf's inscriptions do not relate to any known Egyptian god but phonetically sound "Iouiya", close to Yaouai – a variant of Yahweh. It is noteworthy that Jusuf's grandson, Akhenaten, became Pharaoh and developed the 'One God' concept in Egypt.

11.11 When Amenhotep III became pharaoh, he married his infant sister, Situman, to protect the bloodline and, in order to have an adult wife, he also married Tiye – the daughter of Jusuf. It was decreed that no son of Tiye could inherit the throne, nor could she represent the state god, Amen. Tiye's first son, Tuthmosis did die young, **her second son was sent to be raised by her Israelite relatives at the former Hyksos city of Avaris**. Further details echo the story of Moses. This second son, Amenhotep, born c1394BC, was later educated at Thebes as Tiye became more influential following Situman's failure to produce more than one daughter – Nefertiti. Amenhotep succeeded his father becoming Amenhotep IV, and presumably because of his part Israelite upbringing developed the notion of Aten – the omnipotent god with no image (i.e. no idols were made to represent Aten) – god was represented only by the rays of the Sun. Aten was not the Sun god – that was Ra. Amenhotep (Amen is pleased) changed his name to Akhenaten (Glorious Spirit of

Aten) – Aten being the equivalent of Hebrew Adon, (Lord). The prophesy given to Isaac (Genesis 15.18), that Isaac's issue would reign over the Egyptian Empire (at that time from Egypt to the Euphrates) was thus fulfilled through Akhenaten. However, Akhenaten had threats of armed insurrection if he did not restore the traditional gods to be worshipped alongside the faceless (no idol images) Aten. Akhenaten refused and was forced to abdicate – his followers continued to regard him as the Muse or Mosis. No record has been found of his death nor any burial remains – his burial tomb has been located at Amarna, with unused outer mummy casings with his canopic chest of alabaster jars – empty, unstained and unused. So, it would suggest he fled rather than died. It would seem that this is whom the Bible refers to as "the former Egyptian prince turned prophet".

11.12 In 1939, Sigmund Freud published a theory that the deposed Akhenaten was the one who led a significant number of Israelites out of Egypt when he was deposed. An Egyptian student, Ahmed Osman, also found many close parallels between the recorded upbringing of Moses and of Akhenaten that has led to much debate.

11.13 Akhenaten forbade the worship of other gods, a radical departure from the centuries of Egyptian religious practice. Finally, Akhenaten issued a royal decree that the name Aten was no longer to be depicted by the hieroglyph of a solar disc emanating rays but instead had to be spelled out phonetically. Thus, Akhenaten extended even further the concept of the universal creator god not being a celestial body but a universal spiritual presence. Akhenaten was famous for songs and poems praising Aten, one such, known as the "Great Hymn to Aten" bears an uncanny resemblance to Psalm 104. Psalm 104 is catalogued as written towards the end of David's life in 1015BC – one of the earliest writings in archaic Hebrew, so some textual changes during four or five centuries of oral tradition are hardly surprising.

The Dionysus connection

11.14 Many have observed over the centuries that the tales of Dionysus (Bacchus to the Romans) seem to have been drawn very heavily on the story of Moses. However, now we have solid evidence that the myths of Dionysus are far older than the authorship of Moses – it seems that in reality the story of Moses may have been heavily influenced by the earlier

PART ONE: GOD, ENKI, RA/MARDUK & YAHWEH

stories about Dionysus.

11.15 Dionysus, as a Cretan wine god, has been traced to the introduction of viniculture from Egypt to Crete around 3200BC. As with most things, it pays to look for a Sumerian connection to establish origins. Carl Becker in Modern Theory of Language Evolution, suggests the root name Dionis or Diony found in Egypt and Crete may have gained a suffix from use in Sumeria as the "sus" meaning healing in Sumerian. The Sumerian god of healing being IAUNuShUSh. Intriguingly, from there to Yehoshua (Yah saves) is not a big step linguistically.

11.16 The ancient city of Beit She'an, 30 kms south of the Sea of Galilee in the Jordan Valley, is recorded by ancient historians (including Diodorus and Plutarch) as being founded by Dionysus, as does a plaque dating from Marcus Aurelius c160AD. Archaeological excavations show it was a large town before 2000BC. Between the 15th and 12th Centuries BC it was an important Egyptian administrative centre until the biblical reference to it being occupied by King David around 1030BC. Beit She'an remained an Israelite city until 732BC when conquered by Tiglath Pileser III, the Assyrian king. There is evidence that, throughout this period, Dionysus and many other gods continued to be worshipped. (see jewishvirtuallibrary.org)

11.17 Homer's Iliad and Odyssey both include references to Dionysus but the exact dates these were written are disputed. Estimates for The Iliad range between 750BC and 725BC, whilst its sequel, The Odyssey, is dated between 743BC and 713BC. The Odyssey incorporates many astrological observations, which have been used to calculate the exact date for Odyssey's return – 16 April 1178BC. As the Odyssey relates that this was 10 years after the fall of Troy, suggesting 1188BC – it is noteworthy that the best archaeological estimate of Troy's destruction is 1190BC. It would seem that Homer had very accurate records to draw upon when writing his epics. Suffice to say these two popular tales were already many centuries old when the Hebrews were in exile in Babylon.

11.18 References to Dionysus have been unearthed in Mycenean cities dating back to the 13th century BC. So, by the time the story of the Exodus was written up in Babylon, the myths and legends surrounding the cult of the wine god were legion. Most of the descriptions of Dionysus travels are given in the context of Greek culture and it is not obvious when the stories date back to – but we know the cult of Dionysus originates millennia prior to the Exile. Historians such as Herodotus and Plutarch describe Egyptian worship of Osiris as based upon Dionysus, including both being drawn from the river and both sharing the regular transformation of water into wine. The similarities between the saga of Dionysus, which were clearly understood as elaborate stories, and the purported factual account of Moses role in the Exodus are so extensive it would appear that the Dionysus cult was a major source of inspiration for the Levites writing up the tale of Moses. When reading the stories of Dionysus, one is amazed by the commonalities, some of which are listed below.

- Dionysus is described as "bimater" with birth and adoptive mothers – same as Moses

- One of Dionysus names is 'Nilus' indicating a connection with the Nile

- Another name is 'Mises', rather similar to 'Moses'

- As a baby, Dionysus was drawn out of the waters in a small box

- Dionysus was raised in northern Arabia, as Moses supposedly spent 40 years with Jethro in northern Arabia.

- Dionysus married one of seven planets (Venus) whilst Moses married one of seven sisters (Zipporah)

- When travelling both Moses and Dionysus led their party with a pillar of fire

- Both Moses and Dionysus encountered lands flowing with milk and honey – Dionysus found wine in excess and Moses managed (somehow) to supply large quantities for the priests

- Both Moses and Dionysus used their thyrsus to strike rocks bringing forth fresh water, Dionysus could also bring forth fountains of wine!

- Dionysus had a magical rod wrapped with snakes that he could transform into a serpent, Moses had his staff to part waters and a bronze pole which he could turn into a serpent

- Dionysus used his rod to part the Orontes, the river of the Bekaa Valley, Lebanon, Moses used his rod to part the Red Sea

- Dionysus had Maira - uncannily similar to Moses's Miriam or Maria

- Adopting key Dionysus motifs went as far as copying Dionysus having a dog as a companion into Moses having a companion named Dog (Caleb being Hebrew for 'dog')

- Yahweh gave Moses very detailed instructions on how to butcher animals for sacrifice, Dionysus specified very similar detailed rules but the inspiration here may have just been contemporary priestly practice in Babylon – which even included the use of tiny bells on their tunics and ceremonial smearing of lambs blood on the door lintels of the temple.

- One of the most important Dionysian festivals was the Feast of Bowers to celebrate the grape harvest – Moses copied this in the Feast of the Tabernacles taking place after the grape harvest – although one wonders where the vineyards were? There were no vineyards in Sinai or northern Arabia and Moses died before entering Canaan.

- One of Dionysus epithets was thesmophorus, the lawgiver, and his laws were engraved on two marble tablets. Given the inspiration for the text of the 12 Commandments was the most likely the Book of the Dead, one begins to see the literary endeavors of the Levite priests as aiming to build foundational beliefs from popular contemporary legends.

11.19 To explore these similarities further, I recommend a truly excellent book, "Did Moses Exist?" by D.M. Murdoch which gives far more detailed information concerning these and many other similarities between Dionysus and Moses.

11.20 Given the huge number of similarities, it would seem very clear that the myths and stories about Dionysus greatly influenced the drafting of parts of the Torah in Babylon. The puzzle is why the plagiarism is so blatant, it is quite possible that the priests were deliberately trying to assimilate the worship of Dionysus into that of Yahweh. This process might be a natural progression – look closely and the role of grapes, wine and its use in the first Temple are prominent. Jeremiah 35:2 refers to side chambers within the House of the Lord, to which people were led and given wine. In Song of Songs 2:4, translated to English as "He has taken me to the banqueting hall, and his banner over me is love", the Hebrew *"bayith yayin"* more generally denotes 'wine' rather than 'love' whilst the Septuagint translates the chamber as "house of wine" using "oikos" which also denotes 'temple', as does the Hebrew "bayith". So, Solomon is saying that his lover is brought into the Temple of Wine.

11.21 Plutarch, the famous Greek historian (AD46 to AD120) wrote extensively on his observations of the Jewish festivals and priestly attire, little bells and trumpets, concluding that the Hebrews were worshipping Dionysus. Murdoch identifies numerous historians and theologians who have identified similarities between Moses and Dionysus over the past 500 years (including Voltaire) – most have believed Moses to be the origin and Dionysus copied from his story – mainly as the Old Testament was the only text available that incorporated a detailed historical perspective. However, now it is clear that most of the Torah dates only from c500BC, whilst we have a huge amount of references to Dionysus stretching back into the 3rd Millennium BC – up to a thousand years before Moses was supposed to have lived. The direction of the copying is now clearly from the Dionysus myth into the Moses story. This goes some way to explaining much of the nonsensical detail described in the Torah.

Gilgamesh

11.22 As with Dionysus, the Epic of Gilgamesh appears to be the source of much inspiration to the writers of the Torah. The Gilgamesh story does seem to have an historical core, in that Gilgamesh himself is recorded as a Sumerian king of Uruk around 2700BC. The numerous copies of this Epic across the ensuing centuries down to the period of the Exile some 2,200 years later show how such myths evolve, with later versions supplanting certain original key characters with local deities, such as the Babylonian Marduk. In some ways, the evolution of the Epic could prove a useful example for tracing the evolution of the Torah – except that we do not have written versions of the older oral traditions of the Torah that formed parts of its final written text.

11.23 There are versions of the Epic of Gilgamesh extant in original Sumerian, Akkadian, Babylonian Amorite, Ugarit Canaanite, Hittite, Phoenician and Chaldean. The Epic was very popular, widely used as a school text, including in Ugarit, and read aloud in full as a religious celebration, as in Babylon at the time of the Exile.

11.24 The Hebrew word for Gilgamesh is a combination of the Sun god 'Shamash' and 'Mosheh', resulting in the Hebrew word sounding like "wheel" or "circle of Moses".

11.25 That the Epic of Gilgamesh predates the earliest date ascribed to Moses by a millennium or so is now a given. As with Dionysus, many features of the Gilgamesh epic appear in the story of Moses:

- The hero goes on his quest with his brother – Gilgamesh with Enkidu and Moses with Aaron

- The hero climbs a mountain where he finds god, to whom he offers roast meat

- As Moses spent 40 days on Mt Sinai, Gilgamesh spends 40 days struggling between good and evil

- After meeting with god, the hero returns with a sunburnt face

- Gilgamesh prays to Sin, the Moon god, symbolised as a young bull, as do the Israelites to the Golden Calf representing the god Sin

- Gilgamesh kills the Bull of Heaven as Moses destroys the Golden Calf

- A magical serpent features prominently – both have rods and a bronze snake

- Both stories give prominence to the number 12

- In both stories the hero's brother dies before the quest is attained

- Both Gilgamesh and Moses are described as author of their story

- Both Gilgamesh and Moses supposedly write of their own death

- Gilgamesh fate is determined by Enlil, the senior god (Ruler of Seven), Moses fate determined by Yahweh – who was probably Enlil's son, Nannar (aka Sin)

Again, I recommend Murdock's book "Did Moses Exist?" where she identifies no less than 27 parallels between Gilgamesh and Moses.

11.26 Islamic scholars, including Dr Brannon Wheeler, have also noted use of elements of the Gilgamesh epic in Koranic descriptions, e.g. of events at the well in Midian, but without any reference to Gilgamesh. Indeed, Arabs probably knew the ancient Sumerian hero by the name Masu or Mashu, almost the same as Musa, their name for Moses – and their stories seem to have merged.

Sargon

11.27 The story of the origin of famous King Sargon of Akkad, c2550BC also provides material for the Moses saga. Sargon is recorded as being born of a lowly woman and an unknown father, set adrift in a basket of bulrushes. Sargon was found by Akki, a gardener who brought up the child. Sargon was later identified by the goddess Ishtar and appointed king – founding the first Akkadian dynasty and carving out a combined Sumerian and Akkadian empire covering an area greater than today's Iraq.

Derivation of Moses name

11.28 The Hebrew words for Messiah *'mashiyach'* and the Sun god *'Shamash'* share the same primitive Hebrew root *'mashach'* as does 'mashah' "to draw" conventionally seen as the origin of 'Moses'. The Ugarit term for "anoint" is *'msh'*, whilst its Egyptian equivalent is *'mas'*, *'masu'* or *'mesu'*. The Rev. Archibald Sayce (1845 – 1933), an Assyriologist, asserted that *Mashu* or *Māšu* meaning 'hero', found frequently in Babylonian tablets was the same as Hebrew Moses/Mosheh – and a term applied to Shamash the Sun god. In one of the Amarna tablets, the Pharaoh is addressed as the rising Sun god of the divine day, to which is added "whose name is *Masi*". *Masi* is letter for letter the same as the Hebrew *Mosheh*, for Moses. *Massû* is the Akkadian equivalent and *mas.su* the Sumerian – both meaning "leader".

11.29 The Sumerian *Muš* for serpent, or source of wisdom, gives *Mush* as a moniker for serpent cult founder, as well as *Moses*, *Mosheh* and *Musa* as in Arabic.

11.30 For the Hebrew *Môše*, the association with the Sumerian, and subsequently Canaanite, serpent god seems much more convincing than the pale and banal Egyptian origin being a diminutive of "born". Moses sacred emblems include his serpent wand and bronze serpent on a pole and his tribe is Levi, even the name of the tribe signifies "serpent" (see Michael Astour, *"Hellenosemitica"*, 1967).

11.31 Hence "Mosheh" was an obvious name to apply to the mythical lawgiver, with multiple meanings suitable for the story being developed.

Conclusions

11.32 As an aside, another inconsistency in the tale of Moses concerns the Nephilim. A key reason given in Genesis for God's wrath resulting in the Flood, is the evil wrought by the descendants of the Nephilim, those who 'came down' to Earth and fornicated with the daughters of men. The Flood is supposed to have wiped out all their descendants – yet the scouts sent ahead by Moses into Canaan to spy out the land gave surprising accounts. *All the people we saw there were of great size. We saw the Nephilim there (the descendants of Anak come from the Nephilim). We seemed like grasshoppers in our own eyes, and we looked the same to them.* (Numbers 13:32-33)

11.33 Let us conclude on the historicity of Moses. The mass of evidence suggests that Moses is a mythical composite figure based upon oral traditions recalling a number of leaders – maybe including the leader of the remnants of the defeated Hyksos king, Khamudi, and of the deposed Akhenaten, and probably his chief priests (e.g. character of Aaron) trying to establish a monotheistic religion; with many attributes drawn from Dionysus and Gilgamesh.

11.34 Murdoch observes that the story of Moses and the Exodus can be understood not as literal history or history mythologised but as **myth historicised**. The lawgiver motif ranks as solar and allegorical, reflecting an ancient archetype common to other epic myths including Dionysus, Gilgamesh and Sargon – all of whom were ancient hero's already established for more than a millennium at the supposed time of Moses.

WHO WAS MOSES?

12

Who is God in the Torah?

12.1 The original Hebrew of the Torah is very revealing. Long after the translations for the KJV, we see evidence of that the names employed for God are actually the names of pagan gods echoing many far older Sumerian theological concepts – names that Abraham would have brought with him from Ur.

12.2 El Elyon was the Canaanite name of the Sumerian god ruling the northern hemisphere – Enlil. El Shaddai, as referred to in 11.6 above, may have originally been *śedim* (as written in Deuteronomy 32:17) or *śaday* referring to a mountain or wilderness dweller – suggestive of the Sin (Akkadian name for one of Enlil's sons). In the Sumerian theology, the supreme deity was Anu, his two key sons jostling for the inheritance were Enlil and Enki. Enlil ruled the northern hemisphere and Enki ruled the southern hemisphere, or 'underworld' – in reality, various records indicate Enki is most associated with the continent of Africa. Sumerian records indicate that Enlil and Enki knew in advance of the impending change in sea levels which became immortalised as the Flood. Recent evidence indicates the cause may have been cometary fragments vaporising part of the North American icecap causing a significant change in sea levels. The Sumerian belief was that Enlil was happy to see mankind eradicated but Enki acted to save a few people – as immortalised in the epic of Ziusudra (often referred to by his Babylonian name, Utnapištim).

12.3 Enki was denoted as the wise serpent who wanted to teach mankind skills and persuaded Eve to eat of the Tree of Knowledge. The serpent has, since the Sumerian civilisation, always represented medical wisdom and continues to adorn all representations of doctors, hospitals, etc.. Incidentally, the Tree of Life, the other special tree in the Garden of Eden was probably a grapevine – the Sumerian name for the grapevine is GESH-TIN – literally "tree" + "life".

12.4 Enlil, whose Canaanite names, "El Elyon" and "El Shaddai" echo throughout the Torah, along with the name Yahweh, were translated in code into the KJV of the Bible – as the Most High, the Lord Almighty and the LORD – and are all are treated by contemporary Christians as the descriptions of a single God.

12.5 El Elyon was described in Sumerian theology, as well as in Canaanite tablets found at Ugarit, as having 70 sons (probably better translated as 'descendants') – which is corroborated in Psalm 82. According to rabbinical records, Psalm 82 was written on the appointment of judges by Jehoshaphat in 897BC. In Hebrew, Psalm 82 states *"El Elyon chairs the assembly of the gods, ...Yahweh tells the multitude, you are all gods, you are all sons of El Elyon"*. In Hebrew, Deuteronomy 32.8, states that *"El Elyon, when allocating lands amongst the issue of Adam, identified Yahweh's portion as Jacob's inheritance."* This certainly suggests that El Elyon and Yahweh are two different entities – not one and the same but probably father and son or grandson – which would make Yahweh either Nannar/Sin or Shamash. Both that section of Deuteronomy and Psalm 82 are thought to have been written around 900BC.

12.6 When King David occupied Jerusalem in c1000BC, the pre-existing chief deity of Jerusalem was El Elyon. David introduced the worship of Yahweh and, as recorded in Kings, the Israelites continued to worship other gods as well. A Canaanite clay tablet has been found (Ref KTU 2.4.13-14) which seems to support the biblical statements, the tablet is referred to as the 'Proclamation of Yamm', the text is translated as "And Latipan El the beneficent speaks: the name of my son is Yw and he pronounces the name Yamm". "Latipan El" being another name of El Elyon meaning 'father of mankind', whilst the similarity between Yw and YHWH is suggestive.

12.7 Amongst these 70 sons are Nannar (Sin in Akkadian; Baal in Canaanite and Hebrew) who is recorded as Enlil's first son from Ninlil; and YHW/Yahweh – the chief deity of the Midianites, whose chief priest Jethro, was Moses father in law. So, it appears that Yahweh and Baal were both sons of the Most High, El Elyon. Alternatively, Yahweh may have been just the Israelite name for Sin/Baal. (The number 70 also resonates with the 70 "elders" of Israel who were invited to accompany Moses up Mount Sinai to meet El Elyon. Genesis 24:9).

12.8 It seems likely that writing in Babylon, during the exile around 550BC, the priests compiling the Torah tried to assimilate El Elyon and his more popular successor, Yahweh, into a single god. Evidence for this, and the clumsy way it was done may be shown by:

- The strange dialogue at the Burning Bush in Exodus 3. Here it relates that Moses, supposedly brought up in a devout Israelite family, is told by the Burning Bush that the speaker was the God of Abraham, of Isaac and of Jacob – whom Moses must have known for his 80 year life as El Elyon. Moses then asks what seems a totally superfluous question – "what is your name?" Why indeed would Moses have questioned the identity of the God speaking from the Burning Bush – having just heard the voice explain he was the god of his fathers? One plausible explanation is to fulfil the priestly requirement to link the two powerful gods and subsume them into one. Exodus suggests Moses was not fazed by the new name – neither does it explain whether it is just a new name or a new god – clearly these legitimate questions were not in the minds of the priestly authors! Henceforth in the Torah, the supreme deity is generally referred to as Yahweh and the names El Shaddai / El Elyon are quietly dropped. However, "later" books (Judges, Kings, Psalms) tend to revert to El Elyon and El Shaddai.

- We are told in Exodus that Moses only learned of God's new name of Yahweh when he was 80 years old – it seems a bit odd then that his mother, Jochebed, who must have been born around a 100 years earlier, has a name which in Hebrew reads: "the Honour of Yahweh". Even Yahweh himself confirms in Exodus 6:2-3 that he never revealed that name previously!!

12.9 Whilst bible translations are presented as showing El Elyon and Yahweh as being the same god, it is clear from the Exodus text that Moses assumed they were different (even after being told the latter was the former) and the Israelites continued to treat them as two gods almost until the

PART ONE: GOD, ENKI, RA/MARDUK & YAHWEH

Exile. El Elyon continued to be worshipped by Israelites in the Temple built by Solomon and during the marzeah celebration – the exact meaning of which is disputed but generally thought to be related to celebrations at a funeral. *But by the time of Jeremiah and Amos, the priests regarded El Elyon as a pagan cult and tried to suppress it!!* Amos lived in the Northern Kingdom, prophesying around 760BC – against the setting up by Jeroboam (2nd king of Israel) of the alters at Bethel and Gilgal together with two golden calves representing Baal / Sin, one of El Elyon's sons – so multiple gods were worshipped at both places.

Yahweh's origins

12.10   The oldest possible reference to Yahweh dates from during the reign of Sin-Muballit (c1800BC using the middle chronology), Hammurabi's father, an Amorite king of the First Babylonian empire. The inscription, on a cuneiform tablet states "Yahwe is God" according to a German Assyriologist, Friedrich Delitzsch (1850-1922). Note: the king's name clearly indicates allegiance to Sin rather than Ra/Marduk for whom the city of Babylon was built. This inscription indicates that Yahwe was another name of Nannar/Sin – already used in Babylon 1200 years prior to the Exile!

12.11   The Torah itself suggests Yahweh originated from around Midian, in northern Arabia: bibleinterp.com states: "Not itself indigenous to Palestine, the cult of Yahweh seems first to have developed in 13th century among *Sh3sw* steppe dwellers in the regions of *Seir* and *Midian* (i.e. deep in Sinai, land allocated to Sin). The 9th-century Mesha stele refers to *Yahw* worship at Nebo and a near contemporary inscription from Kuntillat Ajrud associates *"Yahw"* with cult centers in both Samaria and Tawilan (ancient *Teman*). Yahwism's Midian origins may be echoed in the biblical story of Moses, whose father-in-law was a Midianite priest, meeting Yahweh in the burning bush on the "mountain of God" (Exodus 3). Elsewhere, the Bible variously speaks of Yahweh as having come from the Edomite steppe and the desert fringe – from Seir, Paran, Teman, and Midian (Deuteronomy 33:2; Judges 5:4-5; Habakkuk 3:3). So too the Samaritan figure of Yahweh, the god of love, guardian of the stranger in the land and of one in need (Genesis 4:1-16; Leviticus 19:18,34) is very similar to the divine figure of a Nabataean cult reflected in two inscriptions from the caravanserai of Qaryat al-Faw in the Hijaz, which refer to a nameless deity, the divine *wd*, the "beloved", who is represented by the crescent and star and protects the traveller and the stranger, the poor, and the needy."

12.12 There are two Egyptian texts, one dated to the period of Amenophis III (14th century BC), the other to the age of Ramesses II (13th century BC) which refer to 'Yahu in the land of the Šosū-Bedouins', *(t3 š3šw jhw3)*, in which *Yahu* is a toponym (place name). Regarding the Shasu of Yhw, Professor Michael Astour observed that the "hieroglyphic rendering corresponds very precisely to the Hebrew tetragrammaton YHWH, or Yahweh, and antedates the hitherto oldest occurrence of that Divine Name – on the Moabite Stone – by over five hundred years." One hypothesis is that it is reasonable to infer that the demonym (the natives of a place) 'Israel' recorded on the Merneptah Stele refers to a Shasu enclave, and that, since later Biblical tradition portrays Yahweh "coming forth from Se'ir" the Shasu, originally from Moab and northern Edom, went on to form one major element in the amalgam that was to constitute the "Israel" which later established the Kingdom of Israel. Anson Rainey reaches a similar view in his analysis of the el-Amarna letters.

12.13 Professor K. Van Der Toorn concludes that, *"By the 14th century BC,* **before the cult of Yahweh had reached Israel,** *groups of Edomites and Midianites worshipped Yahweh as their god"*. However, the proposed link between the Yahweh of the Israelites and the Shasu is uncertain, given that in the Merneptah reliefs, the group later known as the Israelites are not described or depicted as Shasu. The Shasu are depicted hieroglyphically with a determinative indicating a land not a people.

Frank J. Yurco and Michael G. Hasel distinguish the Shasu in Merneptah's Karnak reliefs from the people of Israel since they wear different clothing, hairstyles, and are determined differently by Egyptian scribes. Moreover, Israel is determined as a people, though not necessarily as a socioethnic group. Egyptian scribes tended to bundle up rather disparate groups of people under one 'artificial unifying rubric'. The most frequent designation for the "foes of Shasu" is the hill-country determinative. Thus they are differentiated from the Canaanites, who are defending the fortified cities of Ashkelon, Gezer, and Yenoam. At the same time, the hill-country determinative is not always used for Shasu, as is the case in the "Shasu of Yhw" name rings from Soleb and Amarah-West. Gösta Werner Ahlström argued that the reason Shasu and Israelites are differentiated from each other in the Merneptah Stele is because these Shasu were nomads while the Israelites were a sedentary subset of the Shasu.

12.14   The demonym 'Israel' can reasonably be referred to as a Shasu enclave, and it can be concluded that the Shasu originated from Moab and northern Edom and eventually helped to constitute the nation of 'Israel' which later established the Kingdom of Israel. The Shasu are mostly depicted hieroglyphically with a determinative indicating a land rather than a people, referencing people of that particular land."

Nannar (Sumerian), Sin (Akkadian), Baal (Canaanite & Hebrew) – represented as the young calf, whose horns (rotated 90°) symbolised a crescent moon

12.15   In Exodus 19.1 it states that the Israelites arrived at the camp before the mountain of God, three months after leaving Egypt, "on that very day". The deeper significance is found in the original Hebrew text of the Torah, which states that they arrived "on the day of the third New Moon after leaving Egypt, on that very day".

12.16   The significance of the day of the New Moon is that Abraham's family originally in the city of Ur, and later in the city of Harran, would have worshipped the local city god, Sin, on the day of each New Moon. This was a day of rest and worship occurring each lunar month, called the "Shabbatu" in Akkadian. So, it is interesting that Moses announced the institution of a weekly "Sabbath" when he descended the mountain with the Tablets – this suggests the writers were more familiar with the weekly day of rest in Babylonian culture than the original Abramaic familiarity of a lunar festival.

12.17   In Numbers 10.10 there is confirmation of continued worship of Sin, despite the destruction of the Golden Calf, where the Hebrew (and some but not all English translations) states that trumpets shall be blown at your (Festivals and) New Moon Feasts – Abraham's descendants continued to observe the Sumerian 'Sabbaoth' worship of Sin every New Moon! One wonders whether this confusion arises from multiple authors or a later, partial process of redaction. Even today, almost 4000 years later, Jews still celebrate the monthly New Moon, the festival of Rosh Chodesh – as the head of the month, a legacy of the worship of the god Sin.

12.18   Sin was the tutelary deity of the city of Ur – the old capital city of the Sumerian empire from which Abraham's family originated and also of many other Mesopotamian cities. The priesthoods read the skies to determine who was the rightful overlord – as precession moved the dominant zodiacal sign from Taurus to Ares, so allegiance was moving from Enlil, signified by the bull, to Ra/Marduk signified by the Ram. But whilst Ra could be characterized as spreading from Egypt, Enlil's firstborn, Nannar/Sin was the local Mesopotamian hero. The importance of Sin was far greater than just a city god, the moon god is clearly one of the most important deities in the wider pantheon of Mesopotamia. In the Early Dynastic god lists, such as Fara SF 1, Sin appears immediately after the four leading gods Anu, Enlil, Enki, and Inanna (Klein 2001: 290).

12.19 The continuity of customs relating to the worship of Sin is staggering. From the Akkadian period until the middle of the Old Babylonian period (roughly 2100BC to 1400BC), the daughter of the reigning king was always appointed to be the high-priestess of Sin (Krebernik 1993-98b: p367-9).

12.20 Beyond the alluvial plains of Mesopotamia, a cult centre of Nannar/Sin is also attested at Harran (just over the border of modern Turkey) where the temple name was é-húl-húl "House of Rejoicing" (Krebernik 1993-98b: 368). At Harran, a long inscription was found on a stele which commemorates Adda-guppi, the mother of Nabonidus, and which celebrates her reverence of Sin. Another stele inscription from Harran describes Nabonidus' accession to the throne, which is here described as being at the will of Sin, and that he rebuilt the é-húl-húl temple (Gadd 1958). Harran is, of course, the city that Abraham's family moved to from Ur.

12.21 In the Sumerian tale Enlil and Ninlil (Etc.SL 1.2.1), Nannar/Sin is described as the first-born son of Enlil and Ninli. So, in the culture from which Abraham came, Sin was the first born of Enlil (whose Canaanite names, "El Elyon" and "El Shaddai" in the Torah refer to God). So, what could be more reasonable for the Israelites, having seemingly lost God and with their leader, Moses, stuck up a mountain for almost 40 days, than to decide to set up an image of God's son, Sin, in his recognized form of a young bull – and cover it with gold leaf?

12.22 Some have equated the golden calf with Baal. Baal was the name of a son of the supreme deity ("El Elyon") in the Canaanite pantheon, also represented as a young bull – but historical references have only been found dating back as far as 1400BC. This suggests that the Canaanite

PART ONE: GOD, ENKI, RA/MARDUK & YAHWEH

deities were indeed derived from the original Sumerian deities.

12.23 Sinai may be translated as the land of, or belonging to, the moon god – "sin-ai". This puzzled me for a while, because the Sumerian records are clear that what we call Sinai today was allocated to NinHarSag, the sister of Enlil and Enki. See Chapter 13 for the biblical and historical solution that I have identified.

12.24 In the Sumerian pantheon, Sin has a son named Shamash (in Akkadian language). Psalm 84.11 gets translated as "the Lord is a sun" or "the Lord is our sun" but the original Hebrew simply states "Shamash is Yahweh" – which can be read as meaning Shamash, the Sumerian sun god, is Yahweh (or vice versa). Shamash being a grandson of Enlil was counted as one of the "70".

12.25 Even the Prophet Mohammed (PbuH) who fervently believed in a single god, relented for a while, when he received divine revelation in the form of sura 53.19-20, to embrace and endorse worship of Al Lat, Al Uzza and Manat, the three daughters of the god symbolized by the Moon, Al Ilah (which does sound awfully close to Allah) by his followers, many of whom had traditionally worshipped Sin. Somewhat later, the exact period is hotly debated by Islamic scholars, Mohammed received a subsequent revelation denouncing worship of Sin's daughters and then stated that it was Satan that had made the first revelation promoting Sin. The two offending verses are known as the Satanic Verses, made notorious by Salman Rushdie.

12.26 The longevity of the influence of Sin can be shown by the inclusion of the symbol of the crescent Moon atop many mosques, on the national flags of no less than 11 Muslim countries (see Algeria, Malaysia, Pakistan, Turkey, etc..) and of course the Muslim country equivalent of the Red Cross being called the Red Crescent.

Asherah (Israelite) / Ashtoreth (Canaanite) from Inanna (Sumerian), Ishtar (Akkadian)

12.27 Inanna (meaning Lady of Heaven), represented as the planet Venus, the goddess of love, fertility and war, was the daughter of Sin (the Moon god) and known as Ishtar in Akkadian and Babylon, Ashtoreth in Canaan, Asherah in Israel and Venus in the Roman pantheon. She was the chief deity of Uruk, a competitor city of Ur. Her consorts varied across time and location, the Hebrews associated her with Baal but she has also been shown as the consort of Yahweh. Which again indicates that Yahweh may just have been the Israelite name for Ba'al/Nannar/Sin. Inscriptions written in Phoenician and archaic Hebrew at Kuntillet Ajrud, dating from around 900BC according to Tel Aviv University archeologists, state "Yahweh and his Asherah" and "Yahweh of Teman and his Asherah", Teman being in Edom, the south east of Canaan and not far from the area inhabited earlier by the Midianites. Teman was also described as an early cult centre for Yahweh in the 13 century BC. Small intertwined figurines of 'Yahweh and his Asherah' have been excavated from many ancient villages across Israel.

12.28 The worship of Asherah was widespread amongst the Israelites, throughout the period from Abraham, including by David and by Solomon, continuing right through to the Babylonian exile – as shown by references to her worship in Deuteronomy 1:4; Joshua 9:10, 12:4, 13:12, Judges 2:13; 1 Samuel 31:10; 1 Kings 11:5; 2 Kings 23:13; 1 Chronicles 6:71; 2 Chronicles 33:19; Jeremiah 7:18; Ezekiel 8:14-15; Micah 5:13-14.

12.29 In 1967, Raphael Patai was the first historian to announce archaeological evidence that indicated the ancient Israelites worshipped both Yahweh and Asherah, who were perceived as a couple. Further research has been conducted by Francesca Stavrakopoulou, a brilliant academic who is a senior lecturer at the University of Exeter. Her research corroborated earlier findings of abundant evidence indicating that the concept of Yahweh having a wife continued during the monarchical period. Stavrakopoulou refers to evidence from Ugarit and from Kuntillet Ajrud in Sinai that, in the 8th century BC, Yahweh and Asherah were prayed to as an item. 2 Kings 21:7 refers to the Temple housing a statue of Asherah.

12.30 Hilkiah, the High Priest, 'found' a Book of the Law (generally believed to be Deuteronomy) somewhere in the Temple in 622BC. After reading it, King Josiah then decided that he had to refurbish Solomon's temple and clear out all the other gods that were being worshipped there – including Baal, Astoreth, "all the starry hosts" and all the priests of these pagan gods. This was followed by the destruction of alters built by Solomon all around the temple and outside Jerusalem at high places for worshipping Ashtoreth, Baal and others, all over Judea.

12.31 Inanna's original Sumerian consort was Dumuzid, known as the Shepherd King, in Sumerian king lists recorded as the fifth king before the Flood !! Listed as the youngest son of Enki, Dumuzi (as known in Egypt) was associated with pastoral activities and initially ruled what is now Sudan. Later, moving to Mesopotamia, Dumuzid was fondly remembered by the Sumerians as the Shepherd King, with numerous references being found to worship and dedications in the 3rd millennium BC. Abraham's family must have sustained worship of Damuzid, bequeathing his descendants memories of the ritual mourning ceremony on the festival commemorating his death. Known as Tammuz to the Israelites, Ezekiel complained of his worship, at the North Gate of the Temple (Ezekiel 8:14-15). Even today, the fourth month of the Jewish calendar is called Tammuz – an amazing feat of recognition for someone who died long before the Flood. Having now found strong historical evidence of a global flood occurring in a narrow date range around 10800BC we can marvel at both the credibility of the Sumerian king-lists and the longevity of the reverence of Tammuz.

12.32 It would seem that following the 'handover' from El Elyon to Yahweh at the Burning Bush, Yahweh was initially understood by the Israelites to be the equivalent of Nannar/Sin, hence their readiness to worship the golden calf. This remained the status quo after settling in Canaan, where the Canaanites worshipped Baal, whose consort was Ashtoreth. The equivalence of Baal and Yahweh may have supported the Israelites belief that Asherah was Yahweh's consort – the fact that Asherah would have been Yahweh's daughter did not present a problem. By the monarchical period, Nannar seems to have given way to his son, with the Israelites recognizing Shamash as their Yahweh, and Asherah continued as consort – as his sister, she was even more acceptable.

12.33 J. Edward Wright, president of The Arizona Center for Judaic Studies and of The Albright Institute for Archaeological Research, notes that although the texts were repeatedly redacted and updated over the centuries, a few such heretical references to Asherah still remain in the Old Testament which confirm her role in the religious beliefs of Israel.

Conclusions

12.34 It would seem that the god of Abraham and his immediate descendants was the most likely to have been the Sumerian chief deity, Enlil, as recorded in the Torah using his Canaanite names, El Elyon and El Shaddai.

12.35 Abraham's followers also worshipped other gods in the Sumerian pantheon, notably Enlil's granddaughter, Inanna (whom they knew as Asherah) and her consort Tammuz, and two of El Elyon's 70 sons, Sin and Yahweh (adopted from the Midianites).

12.36 Adjusting for the late canonisation of most of the books of the Old Testament, it would appear that the Israelites were definitely polytheistic for a thousand years after Moses was supposed to have lived and that the main effort to switch to a monotheism actually took place from the sixth century BC starting with the "discovery" of Deuteronomy and sustained by the creation of the complete Torah in Babylon during the Exile. Only with the remnants returning from Babylon, such as Ezra, was monotheism really established in Israel.

12.37 The circumstances of the struggle to promote Yahweh leading up to the Exile helps explain the masterplan prepared by the priests in Babylon to create a foundation myth and redemption plan for the Israelites who sought forgiveness and re-establishment in what was promoted as the Promised Land. Leviticus, generally thought to date from the Exile or later, clearly reflects efforts by the Kohanite priests to establish control over the Hebrew population, mainly through fear and ritual – including liberal adoption of Babylonian sacrifice and worship rituals. The Priests awarded themselves authority to cut individuals off from God and to banish members of the congregation from the 'settlement' – to separate them from the community – pretty fearsome weapons. Centuries later, the Catholic Church adopted a similar tactic – vesting the Pope with the authority to excommunicate individuals committing them to everlasting damnation in hell. And, in case people felt they could still enjoy the rest of their life on earth, the process could be accelerated by the such persons being also condemned to death by burning at the stake.

12.38 To exert control over the population, and ensure maximum yields, all sacrificial offering had to be centralised, and all offerings passed to the priests. This realised the attraction of Akhenaten's monotheistic creed, removing all competitor gods and any claims they might have on offerings. To consolidate previous separate gods, it was recorded that God had announced he had a new name (Yahweh) and all the previous gods were

PART ONE: GOD, ENKI, RA/MARDUK & YAHWEH

collectivised by adopting a plurality as God's name (Elohim). Kingship had only provided weak and idolatrous leaders – so it was written that the priests would be in charge, and a fearsome God could only be placated through the Priests and by sacrificial offerings. The subjugation of kingship was cemented by the priest messiah being defined as having authority over the king messiah.

12.39 The detailed instructions for ritual cleansing and sacrifices written in Leviticus echo detailed instructions found on Babylonian clay tablets followed by the pagan priests. Four tablets, ANET 331 – 334, describe the order of events for the New Year festival, in the month of Nisan (the Hebrews also copy this Babylonian name of the month from their Exile). The sequences of different sacrifices, recital of prayers, ritual washing and purification, decapitations of animals, incantations, the animal waste being taken outside the city to open country where those bearing it must remain for seven days. The priest's assistant had to take the blood of the sacrificial ram and smear it on the portal and lintels of the palace gateway. (See Hugh Chisholm, Encyclopaedia Britannica page 22.317). Given that Leviticus is believed to have been written entirely during or after the Exile (see section 7), the source of inspiration is clear.

12.40 The extremely tedious rituals for different types of sacrifices set out in Leviticus, are clearly inspired by the ritual animal sacrifices the Kohanite priests would have witnessed being performed for pagan gods – probably just made more elaborate and with added elements of superstition – ritual sprinkling of blood seven times on the altar; "daubing blood on the ear lobe of the right ear, the thumb of the right hand and the big toe of the right foot" (Leviticus 8:23). After reading this it is hardly credible to claim Yahweh is the Creator God – rituals prescribed for Yahweh are almost indistinguishable from rituals for gods such as Sin and Baal. Plainly, the awesome God who designed the formulae controlling the cosmos and the evolution of life as described in sections 2 and 3 of this thesis would not be interested in the superstitious pagan rituals described in Leviticus – and also, as the Bible itself tells us, neither was Jesus.

Further speculation

12.41 The title is deliberate.

12.42 If one reads the story of Moses objectively with today's knowledge, one is tempted to consider whether Yahweh was an extra-terrestrial. As referred to earlier, he exhibited many humanoid traits, clearly adored the aroma of roasted meats, but maybe was allergic to yeast as he repeatedly forbade its inclusion in offerings. The instructions concerning burnt sacrificial offerings to generate "aromas pleasing to the Lord" border on obsession – with instructions in Genesis, Exodus, Leviticus (16 times) and Numbers (18 times). He was also obsessive about details concerning the rituals, sacrifices, curtains, tassels, etc.., and he wanted the light kept on all the time in his dark tent. His appearance might be explained by use of an exo-skeleton, maybe of polished unpainted aluminium (very bright) with a jet-pack strapped on his back to create a pillar of smoke and fire. His 'lander' might have emitted dangerous rays burning up those who got too close and giving radiation burns to survivors – the cause of Moses sun tanned face.

12.43 At first glance, when we read about the large numbers of pagan gods, some with familiar names, that each ancient civilisation worshipped – we exhibit a knee jerk reaction to dismiss them as pagan myths. However, closer examination reveals something interesting – these pantheons generally had clear family relationships between their members. Moreover if one traces the Mesopotamian gods over time, one sees the local names change through the succeeding empires but their key attributes, symbols and family relationships endure – from Sumerian, through Akkadian, Amorite Babylonian, Assyrian, Chaldean Neo Babylonian, Persian, to Greek and Roman before being displaced by Jesus. The longevity and tenacity is surprising – worship of Tammuz, as referred to previously, seems to have survived for more than 11,000 years!

12.44 Why did these Mesopotamian pagan gods survive so long? And why did human civilisation flower so spectacularly in Sumeria with such amazing knowledge of farming, horticulture, animal husbandry, mathematics, astronomy, etc.. Much of this knowledge was gradually lost over the succeeding civilisations until the Romans believed the earth was flat and all the stars revolved around our earth? Many, unfortunately mostly crackpots, speculate that the inspiration for the Sumerian civilisation and for the pantheon of Sumerian gods were in fact visiting extra-terrestrials. If Earth was visited today, we have sufficient technical knowledge to understand such an event – without calling such visitors 'gods'. But, even 200 years ago, before the advent of railroads, how would humans have described something clad in a shimmering metallic 'coat' emerging from a pillar of cloud and smoke which had descended from the heavens?

PART ONE: GOD, ENKI, RA/MARDUK & YAHWEH

12.45 As we considered in the Prequel to this series, the alternative explanation is that a few survivors from an antediluvian civilisation managed to sustain an elite leadership over the new cultures they managed to bring forth. There are even possible explanations for the perceived longevity of their lives – which I have saved for Part Four!

WHO IS GOD IN THE TORAH?

13

Modern maps show Sinai in the wrong place

13.1 Biblical Sinai is NOT where Sinai is shown on maps today but in Northern Arabia.

13.2 The Bible, in several places, states that Yahweh came from Tayma and/or Sinai was in Arabia:-

- Deuteronomy says "the Lord came from Sinai, and rose up from Se'ir unto them; He shined forth from Mount Paran" (Deuteronomy 33:2). In 1 Samuel 25:1 David goes to the wilderness of Paran, presumably thinking that being closer to Yahweh he would be safer from Saul.

- Judges 5:4 – "Lord, when thou went out of Se'ir, when thou marched out of Edom"

- Habakkuk 3:1-3 says that "God comes from Teman" (an early name for Tayma, derived from one of Ishmael's sons), "the Holy One from Mount Paran".

- Galatians 4:24-25 says that Mount Sinai is in Arabia

13.3 Tayma is a large oasis thought to have been inhabited for more than 4000 years, a marker from Ramesses III dated c1180BC has been excavated and the Assyrian king, Tiglath-pileser III, recorded receipt of tribute from Tayma c740BC, whilst after the Roman destruction of the

Jerusalem temple in AD70, Tayma became known as a mainly Jewish town.

13.4 Interestingly there are a number of 8th century BC inscriptions that identify the city of Tayma as a cult centre of Yahweh (see Meshel, Ze'ev, on www.fas.harvard.edu 2007, and Smith, Mark, The Early History of God, 2002, p. 32).

13.5 The idea that Moses fled Egypt to the *present day location of* Sinai – is very problematical. Firstly, when "Moses" fled Egypt (assuming that he was wanted for murder) he would NOT try to hide in the "Sinai" Peninsula where the Egyptians operated many mines and deployed a significant military presence to protect the mines and guard Egypt's eastern frontiers. The biblical story, and logic, indicates Moses fled somewhere beyond Egypt's control.

13.6 Secondly, the name of the man with seven daughters that Moses stayed with, "Jethro", tells us a lot about the location of the place Moses fled to. "Jethro" is a corruption of the Hebrew YATRO coming from the stem "YOD TAW ROSH" the meaning of which is "abundance," and "excess". Protagonists and antagonists in Biblical mythologies generally carry names descriptive of the function they played in life, or in the particular Biblical story that they are featured in. So, the "father-in-law" of "Moses" was a "man of abundance" who perhaps had an excess of wealth and/or flocks, hence the name YATRO. It would be pretty hard to be a man of abundance and have excess wealth and flocks in a place like the "Sinai" Peninsula. However, it would not be so difficult to be a man of abundance if one lived much further east, namely the plains of northern Arabia.

13.7 Jethro lived in the "Land of the Midianites". "Midianite" is derived from the Arabic MIDAN meaning "plains" which describes the geography of northern Arabia from Tayma through Adammatu (Biblical Dumah), Sakkaka, and Ar'ar. This area is sitting on top of a huge aquifer which supplies the wells that have fed the above-mentioned cities for thousands of years. Also, spring rains cause the entire region to burst into a riot of colours as flowers seem to spring up out of nowhere to blanket the countryside from one end to the other (even today). Hence, northern Arabia was the right environment for someone like "Jethro" to become "Mr. Abundance," and would have been an ideal place for someone like